The Hip Guide to Helsinki

Katja Pantzar

with photos by Katja Turunen

THE *HipGuide*
TO HELSINKI

Werner Söderström Osakeyhtiö

Helsinki

ISBN 951-0-27963-3

Painopaikka Ws Bookwell, Porvoo 2003

Contents

Hip 1. characterised by a keen informed awareness of or involvement in the newest, developments or styles. **2.** understanding, aware. **3.** following the latest fashion especially in jazz music, clothes, etc.; stylish. **4.** introducing a united cheer.

- THE OXFORD ENGLISH DICTIONARY

Intro

Hip

Hip is a state of mind. It's knowing your Gap from your Gucci — or in this case, your H&M from your Marimekko — but it doesn't mean that you need to have a closet full of both. It's knowing where to go in Helsinki for good cheap eats or a splashy five-star meal, where to score slick Finnish design from Aalto to Arabia and Iittala, and which bar you're most likely to run into legendary filmmaker Aki Kaurismäki. And it's also knowing a bit about the city's culture and history so that you're savvy to the parodies of Russians and Swedes, and the inside jokes about drinking.

Age is irrelevant when it comes to being hip. My uncle, who is in his 50s and knows all of Helsinki's coolest cafés and the best cycling routes around town, is just as hip as the style-conscious 20-somethings who shop at IvanaHelsinki and sip beer at Erottaja Bar while listening to DJs spin vinyl.

Helsinki's unique charm comes from Finland's cultural and geographic position between Russia and Western Europe, which gives the Nordic city a vibe all of its own. Built on a series of islands and peninsulas jutting into the Baltic, the city's cobble-stoned streets curve around bays and harbours. Most of the capital city's major cultural attractions, from architecturally significant buildings such as Finlandia Hall and Kiasma, the Museum of Contemporary Art, to the neo-classical splendour of Senate Square, are all within walking distance of each other.

A lot of visitor info is available in English, yet few guides go beyond the touristy basics. If you don't speak Finnish or Swedish (the country's other official language), or haven't got friends here, you're out of the loop about what's going on beneath the city's sightseeing surface.

After reading too many awkwardly translated texts and outdated guides that brimmed with misinformation, I

knew that I had to write this book. For in those brochures I couldn't see the Helsinki that I know — a vibrant cosmopolitan metropolis full of innovative design, fusion cuisine, fabulous live music, and distinctive features such as sauna, Sibelius, and *sisu*.

Helsinki is quite safe and generally accessible, whether you're 16 years old or 61 years young. Regardless of budget, you can have a good time. It's also a relatively egalitarian place where you just might find yourself walking by President Tarja Halonen on the street, or bump into top Finnish model Ninja Sarasalo (the face of Jean Paul Gaultier) while browsing through the magazine racks at one of the city's many bookstores.

So whether you're here for two days, two weeks, or two months, I hope this guide helps you make the most of Helsinki.

Katja Pantzar
Helsinki 2003

1.

Helsinki, Finland: A Primer

A City of Contrasts Helsinki is a city of extremes, starting with the dramatically changing light and weather, both of which have a profound effect on the people and the character of the city. Owing to Finland's geographic location — it's Western Europe's northernmost country — Helsinki has 24 hours of daylight at midsummer and just a few hours of light during the darkest depths of winter.

On a perfect summer day, endless sunlight bathes the city in a lemony orange glow. Trees and flowers are in full bloom and the Baltic Sea surrounding Helsinki is warm enough to swim in. People wear brightly coloured clothing, they're friendly and outgoing, and the city is full of bikes as just about everybody cycles to work and play. Every night the city's patios brim with revellers and laughter; numerous concerts and festivals are on around town.

The Power of Light When winter comes, Finns seem to go into hibernation. The happy hues and cottons of summer are replaced with heavy coats and wools in black, gray, and brown. The city grows quiet, as though its inhabitants are resting up for the summer.

British writer and comedian Neil Hardwick, a longtime Helsinki resident, dubbed this seasonal switch "The Winter Rules." The rules, which unofficially kick in on October 1 and run until April, require that people no longer smile, make eye contact with strangers, or wear anything colourful.

While tongue-in-cheek, Hardwick's observations are apt. Curiously, Helsinkians seem to suffer the misconception that their winter is the harshest and cruellest in the world — it's not — and they fall into a collective funk about it.

Summer is undoubtedly an easier season, but winter offers its own charms. During November, December, and January, the city is illuminated with light art and installations. People ski, skate, and take up other winter hobbies such as Nordic walking, which is a kind of power walking using cross-country ski poles.

Helsinki's sharp contrasts are not just a result of geography and climate; history has also left an indelible mark.

Finland: A Very Brief History The first crusade to Finland was led by Swedish King Eric IX in 1155, and for the next 650 years, Finland was part of Sweden. (This partly ex-

plains why Finns are so competitive — in a healthy way, of course — with their Nordic neighbour in every arena from hockey to mobile phone manufacturing.)

In 1809, Sweden lost Finland to Russia, and Finland became a Grand Duchy of the Russian Empire. Independence, which Finns are fiercely proud of, was gained in 1917.

During the Second World War, Finland successfully defended its freedom and fought off invasions by the Soviet Union and Germany. True to its reputation of keeping promises, Finland was the only country to pay off its war reparation debts to the US following the Second World War. Both world wars took heavy financial, political, and psychological tolls on the country, and Finland was re-building its infrastructure until the 1950s. It was then that Finland shifted into high gear. In less than a decade, it moved from an agrarian to an industrial economy.

For much of the 20th century, Finland's foreign policy and careful neutrality were shaped by its relations with its formidable next-door neighbour, the Soviet Union. Finland was a bridge between East and West, and Helsinki an espionage capital during the Cold War. With the collapse of the Soviet Union in the early 1990s, Finland lost its largest trading partner and experienced a severe recession, but was able to step out of the Cold War shadow.

Today Finland is one of the world leaders in technology, and tops global rankings in environmental protection, social security, and education.

Helsinki

In 1550, King Gustav Vasa of Sweden founded Helsinki as a trading post and competitor to Tallinn, the capital of Estonia. Helsinki became the Finnish capital in 1812.

Today Helsinki is home to half a million people, while the metropolitan area has a population of 1 million. In 2000, Helsinki celebrated its 450th anniversary and was one of the nine European Capitals of Culture.

Politics

Reflecting the pursuit of equality for all of its citizens, Finland was the first country in Europe to give women the vote, which it did back in 1906. Finland joined the UN in 1955 and the European Union in 1995.

The major political parties are the Centre Party, the Social Democrats, and the National Coalition. The president is elected by direct popular vote for a term of six years. President Tarja Halonen is in office until 2006. With a female head of state, and about 40 per cent of parliament made up of women, equality is not just a buzzword. Yet, on average, women in Finland still earn less than men.

Numbers The population of Finland is 5.2 million. The official languages are Finnish and Swedish, though most Finnish-speaking Finns speak better English than Swedish. In Helsinki, 88 per cent of the population is Finnish speaking and about 6 per cent of the population is Swedish speaking. Street signs, official notices, labels, and most ads are in both languages.

In Finland there are 2 million saunas.

One of the indigenous languages is Sámi, formerly referred to as Lappish, which is spoken by approximately half of the 6,500 Sámi who live, for the most part, in northern Finland — also known as Lapland.

About 88 per cent of Finland's population belong to the Evangelical Lutheran Church and about 1 per cent belong to the Orthodox Church: Both are designated as state churches.

There are close to 100,000 foreigners in Finland (most live in the Helsinki area), which may not sound like much, but given that ten years ago there were only 33,000 foreigners, it's significant. More than a fifth are from Russia; Estonians and Swedes make up the next largest groups of new immigrants.

In Finland there are 2 million saunas. The average Finn drinks 72 litres of beer per year. Eighty per cent of the population has a mobile phone, and 80 per cent own their own apartment or home.

Geography and Weather Finland is located between the 60th and 70th parallels of latitude, and shares borders with Sweden, Norway, and Russia. Forest covers three quarters of the land surface area, making Finland the most densely forested country in Europe. Often called "the country of a thousand lakes," Finland is truly that: There are more than

180,000 lakes. The 338,000 square-kilometre country also has more islands than any other country in the world.

While Finland has a reputation as a cold place, the Gulf Stream keeps the Scandinavian climate relatively mild. The average temperature is warmer than in American and Asian regions at similar latitudes.

In Helsinki, temperatures in the winter can be as cold as minus 20 or 25 degrees Celsius, though such dips are sporadic. In the summertime, the temperature can be between 10 and 30 degrees Celsius. Summer 2002 was the hottest on record in a hundred years, with numerous days that were 30 degrees Celsius and above throughout the country.

Finnish 101

It's been said that if Finnish is not your mother tongue, it's as difficult to learn as Chinese. Officially, Finnish is a Finno-Ugric language, related to Hungarian and Estonian, with the oldest Finnish words dating back 5,000 years. Encyclopaedia-length words, double consonants, and vowels are plentiful. Place the emphasis on the wrong syllable and the meaning changes entirely — *kaapeli* means "cable" and *kappeli* means "chapel."

Finnish, which is completely phonetic, has 15 grammatical cases whereas contemporary English has essentially two cases, nominative and genitive. There are no pronouns for "he" or "she" as Finnish is gender neutral: *Hän* means "he" or "she," which explains why Finns sometimes muddle their he's and she's in English.

Media, technology, and advertising lingo have influenced the language. You'll recognise words like "e-mail," "video," and "city." Some of the older slang can be traced back to Russian and Swedish, but these days most loanwords come from English.

From Cradle to Grave Although the social welfare system has undergone change in recent years (many Finns feel that it has eroded), Finland still boasts one of the best social systems in the world. Regardless of what you earn, you can still receive a virtually free education, live in standard housing, and get affordable medical care and other social benefits.

> ## "The Finns are silent in two languages."
>
> BERTHOLD BRECHT

One the most visible signs of change is that for the first time ever there are homeless people in Helsinki. This runs counter to the fundamental idea of the welfare state in which every citizen's basic needs should be met.

In recent years, a private medical system that is partly funded by the state has emerged. Both the private and the public systems are still quite moderately priced compared with the cost of similar services in, for example, the United States.

Paid maternity/paternity leaves are standard benefits, and organised childcare is largely paid for by the state. Consequently, the tax rate is higher than in non-welfare countries.

The average working Finn is entitled to five weeks paid holiday a year.

Economy   Finland has a highly industrialised, largely free market economy: Metal, engineering, and electronics account for 50 per cent of export revenues, and forest products for 30 per cent. In 2001, the GDP was 133 billion euros; the GDP per capita was 25, 707 euros. Finland is the only Nordic EU member to adopt the euro as the national currency.

High-Tech Turnaround   When Finland emerged from the recession of the early '90s, it did so with the help of its newly minted European Union membership and a savvy company called Nokia.

Many Finnish companies and people have made a major mark on global technology — think open source software guru Linus Torvalds, the man behind the Linux Operating System. But Nokia, the world's number one mobile phone maker, is without a doubt Finland's biggest international success story to date. It's estimated that 4.5 Nokia phones are sold every second in the world. More than 60 per cent of the Helsinki Stock Exchange runs on Nokia activity.

The explanation for Finland's accelerated high-tech performance? Long before the concept of the global village became a reality, developing communications technology was a priority for Finland, a country geographically and linguistically on the periphery. The mobile phone is the quintessential Finnish design object, exemplifying the concept of form follows function: It's stylish, portable, high-tech, multi-tasking, and efficient.

Wired Finland is one of the world's top users of the Internet, for just about every business, person, and organisation has a functional website. Most banking transactions are done online (paper cheques were made redundant several decades ago); even library books can be renewed online. Text messaging has been a way of life since the mid '90s, and tram tickets and other items can be purchased by mobile phone.

The People In general, Finns work hard and play hard. They are modest, pragmatic, and often humble. Many are unaware of their cultural and historical riches, and don't realise that they are among the best-educated, best-housed, and most well-off citizens in the world.

German playwright Berthold Brecht once noted that "the Finns are silent in two languages." Brecht's oft-repeated remark still holds true: Small talk is not something that Finns excel at — until they've had a few drinks.

Finns have been voted among the most honest people in the world and there's some truth (no pun intended) to that, especially with regard to sincerity of behaviour. If you're invited out for coffee or a meal, it's usually a genuine offer, unlike in some cultures where "we should do coffee" can mean sometimes-maybe-never.

Other sweeping generalisations worth repeating: Many Finns, both spectators and athletes alike, are sports fans. Most appreciate the wilderness. Owing to *jokamiehen-oikeus* or "every person's right," every citizen has access to the land (as long as there's no fence around it), for walking, hiking, or camping, regardless of who owns it. You don't have to ask permission, but implicit in this privilege is respect for the property and its owner's peace and privacy.

And perhaps because Finns have faced adversity throughout their history, they've cultivated a character-defining strength, or persistent determination called *sisu,* which stands for a unique quality that combines spirit and strength.

A Few Famous Finns Well-known Finns on the world stage include 20th-century composer Jean Sibelius, architects Alvar Aalto and Eliel Saarinen, and long distance runner Paavo Nurmi, who won nine gold and three silver Olympic medals during his career.

More recently, the internationally buzzed-about

23

include conductors Esa-Pekka Salonen, Jukka-Pekka Saraste, and Osmo Vänskä; opera singers Karita Mattila and Monica Groop; composer Kaija Saariaho; clothier Peter Nygård; hockey players Teemu Selänne, Jari Kurri, and Christian Ruuttu; race car drivers Mika Häkkinen, Marcus Grönhölm, and young Kimi Räikkönen; skiers Matti Nykänen and slalom champion Kalle Palander; designers Eero Aarnio, Kaisa Blomstedt, and Stefan Lindfors; and Hollywood director Renny Harlin (*Die Hard 2, Cliffhanger,* and *Deep Blue Sea*).

Avant-garde filmmaker Aki Kaurismäki (whose poignant *Man Without a Past* won the Palme D'Or at the 2002 Cannes Festival and was nominated for an Oscar for best foreign film), techno-accordionist Kimmo Pohjonen, and violinist Linda Lampenius (whose dubious distinctions include being the only classical violinist to bare all for *Playboy*) are also well known abroad. On the pop music front, rock bands Leningrad Cowboys, HIM, Hanoi Rocks, and 22 Pistepirkko, along with music meisters Jimi Tenor and NuSpirit Helsinki are just a few of the names recognised worldwide.

Myths Polar bears don't roam the streets of Helsinki. In fact, you'd be hard pressed to find them in any part of Finland, as they're not indigenous. Lapland is not a reindeer-filled theme park in Helsinki, it's a region near the North Pole, a good hour and a half flight from Helsinki. Nokia is not a Japanese company. Saunas are not about sex, they're about health, relaxation, and cleansing. Finland is not so far away: By plane, it's less than three hours from London (closer than the distance between New York and London), less than an hour from Stockholm, and less than two hours from Moscow. Not all Finns are heavy drinkers or good skiers by birthright. Despite reports that the world's last natural blonde will be Finnish, not all Finns are blonde-haired and blue-eyed: Brunettes live here, too.

Hip Helsinki, Exotic Finland

By the year 2000, Helsinki's (and indeed Finland's) international reputation as a cold, dull, expensive place was fast fading.

The old image of a dark, depressing city portrayed in films such as Jim Jarmusch's *Night on Earth,* which features two Helsinki drunks so inebriated that they pass out during a mid-winter cab ride, or as a stand-in for Russia in movies such as *White Nights* (1985), *Gorky Park* (1983), *Reds* (1981), and *Dr. Zhivago* (1965) was being replaced by a very different picture.

Articles about high-tech Nokia Finland peppered the international news media in publications ranging from the venerable *New Yorker* magazine and the *Washington Post* to techie guide *Wired.* Enthusiastic, almost gushy, travel features appeared in British newspapers the *Observer* and the *Guardian;* post-millennium, the British edition of fashion magazine *Elle* named Helsinki the latest chic destination for the international jet set. *Scandinavian Living,* a sort of Nordic *Wallpaper** magazine, ran an extensive cover story extolling the design virtues of hip Helsinki and exotic Finland.

More foreigners had come to visit and some to stay. Helsinki's peoplescape started looking more cosmopolitan: Finns were no longer fair-skinned by default. New ethnic restaurants and bars opened up. Prices came down and people went out more.

As the denizens of hip officially declared Helsinki the latest cold place to become hot, jetting to Helsinki became an in-thing to do, because it was a city full of leading-edge design, music festivals, and fusion cuisine, a mix of the exotic and the familiar. And not so very far away anymore.

info

PLEASE NOTE As in life, everything is subject to change. Cool places close, menus change, and prices go up.

Helsinki uses the 24-hour clock. Thus 4 pm is 16:00, 8 pm is 20:00, and so on. But when locals provide time-related info in English — which most Helsinkians speak well — they'll often use the 12-hour clock.

In general, Helsinki's prices are cheaper than London or New York's. For the most part, the further the café or bar is from the centre of town, the cheaper drinks and food are. Tax and tip are included in the price. The Finnish currency is the euro (€); 1 euro is roughly equivalent to 1 US dollar.

Just about every Finnish business has a website, but not all of them list information in English. For the most part, the websites listed herein have English-language components.

For place names, English names are given if they are commonly used; otherwise the Finnish name is supplied.

For information about the Helsinki Card (www.helsinkicard.com), which offers discounts on museum and gallery entrance fees, transportation and sightseeing, and for details about a variety of other visitor-friendly services, please refer to the book's final section, **Practical Information**. Important phone numbers and useful info regarding maps, transportation, and media are also included in the section.

2.
Cafés

Coffee Time Finns drink the most coffee per capita in the world, an average of four to five cups a day. And Helsinkians get caffeinated in sophisticated surroundings ranging from the sleek modernism of Café Aalto to tony Café Strindberg, or one of the more laid-back spots such as Wayne's Coffee, a sort of Scandinavian Starbucks.

A word to those used to the weaker coffee served in North America and Britain: Finns drink strong — sometimes espresso voltage — black coffee. Most cafés also serve milder blends of coffees, as well as lattés, cappuccinos, and teas. In addition to beverages, sandwiches, pastries, soups, and salads are available.

For a traditional Finnish treat, sample some *pulla*, a pastry-like sweet bread made with cardamom.

Finns drink the most coffee in the world.

Literary Cafés The Esplanade (*Esplanadi*, or *Espa* as it's nicknamed by the locals) is the most picturesque — and touristy — boulevard in the city. Many of the top boutiques and design stores, including the Marimekko flagship store, line the Esplanade, which was once a political dividing line: Finnish-speaking Finns walked on the south side (Eteläesplanadi) and Swedish-speaking Finns on the north (Pohjoisesplanadi). The city's only five-star hotel, the über-swanky Hotel Kämp, is here.

A spacious boulevard park runs between the north and south Esplanade for several blocks, and opposite the park's Kappeli brasserie, there's an outdoor bandstand that hosts free rock, jazz, and classical concerts during the summer.

Along the Esplanade, you'll find the city's greatest concentration of top-notch cafés and brasseries. Walking down the sidewalk café-lined street in the summertime, you could be in any European city, what with the cosmopolitan crowd and the mix of impressive neo-classical buildings.

CAFÉ AALTO (Pohjoisesplanadi 39/+358.9.121.4446) is on the second floor of the Academic Bookstore, which was designed by internationally acclaimed architect Alvar Aalto and his second wife, architect Elissa Aalto, in 1969. With its sleek functionalist design rendered in white marble and its central location, Café Aalto is a favourite spot for book-loving Finns: The country produces more books and magazines per capita than any other country in the world.

The ever-bustling Academic Bookstore is Finland's largest. It stocks about one million titles, and carries 3,000 different newspapers and magazines in 20 different languages including English, German, and French. Among the literary luminaries who have autographed books here: Margaret Atwood, Umberto Eco, Paulo Coelho, Faye Weldon, James Clavell, and Liv Ullman.

Further down the street is **CAFÉ STRINDBERG (Pohjoisesplanadi 33/+358.9.681.20.30)**, overlooking the Esplanade Park. An excellent spot for people watching, its summer patio with its wicker chairs evokes Paris, and the patrons are just as stylish. Marimekko-clad creative types mix with well-heeled 40-something women sporting Burberry bags and Shih-Tzu lap dogs.

Named after the broody Swedish playwright and novelist, Café Strindberg is anything but moody. The upscale brasserie is a great place for a bite to eat or a drink. Upstairs, the second-floor library café-bar, with its huge comfy leather armchairs and oversize couches, is well suited to long philosophical discussions over red wine. If you're travelling solo, you can tuck into the broad selection of magazines including *Vogue* and *Wallpaper**, and watch the beautiful people go by. In the adjacent second-floor restaurant, the city's social swans dine.

For a more casual atmosphere and less expensive eats, **CAFÉ ESPLANAD (Pohjoisesplandi 37/+358.9.665.496)** is one of the city's most popular cafés. Around lunchtime, between 11 am and 2 or 3 pm, there's often a long queue snaking out onto the sidewalk partly because of the café's scrumptious *korvapuusti pulla,* which are like massive cinnamon buns without the icing, and are baked several times a day. At less than 4 euros, Esplanad's *korvapuusti* and coffee (as many refills as you can drink) is one of the best deals in town. The generous mealsize chicken, salmon, and vegetable salads are also good value for money. For less of a line-up and a quick *pulla* fix (Esplanad's *pulla* is truly addictive), try their **PICK UP DELI (Aleksanterinkatu 50/+358.9.676.086)**, which despite a name that makes it sound like a bar for, well, picking up a date, is really just a takeaway deli. **SUCCÉS CAFÉ & BAKERY (Korkeavuorenkatu 2/ +358.9.633.414)**, in the posh Eira neighbourhood, is under the same ownership as Esplanad and Pick Up, and offers similar fare.

CAFÉ KAFKA (Pohjoisesplanadi 2/+358.9.171.380) in the Swedish Theatre (Svenska Teattern), the round white building just across from Stockmann's department store, is frequented by foreigners, theatre-goers, and well-read types. The café, which closes relatively early (at 7 pm), carries an interesting mix of books and magazines including the *Bluffers Guide* series, a kind of Coles/Cliffs notes to essential topics such as law, philosophy, women, men, and whiskey.

Not officially on the Esplanade, but just a block away is **CAFÉ ENGEL (Aleksanterinkatu 26/+358.9.652.776)**, across from Senate Square. Given its close proximity to the University of Helsinki, it's frequented by the thinky creative crowd, as well as tourists, shoppers, and locals. The cosy main room has a narrow hallway that leads to the piano room (*pianohuone*), a well-lit sanctum that looks out over the café's inner courtyard, where arthouse films are shown throughout the summer and on the Night of the Arts festival in late August.

Coffee Casual

Part of a Swedish chain, **WAYNE'S COFFEE (Kaisaniemenkatu 3/+358.9.6843.2310)**, doubles as a Scandinavian Starbucks. The spacious modern interior has a relaxed atmosphere, cool background music, and Wayne's sells a selection of hot and cold beverages, baked goods, sandwiches, and wraps, along with healthy fruit smoothies. There's also a computer with free Internet access for patrons.

MODESTY COFFEE SHOP (Tennis Palace, Fredrikinkatu 65/ +358.9.694.1284 and Sanomatalo, Alvar Aallonkuja 2/+358.9.622.2007)

has a similar youngish urban bent. Its Sanomatalo location is popular with moms of all ages because you can easily push a pram into the ground floor café and there's plenty of room around the tables.

Roberts Coffee is your basic coffee bar with several locations around town including **NET CUP** (Aleksanterinkatu 52/ +358.9.121.3759) on the ground level of Stockmann's department store, with Internet access for café customers. **KAFFECENTRALEN** (Yrjönkatu 30/+358.9.2600.220) offers java connoisseurs a good selection of fine Italian espressos and coffees including Danesi and Monteriva.

MBAR (Mannerheimintie 22-24/+358.9.612.45420) in the Lasipalatsi complex is a lively café-bar with more than a dozen computers with Internet access (1 euro for 10 minutes; 5 euros for an hour).

Artsy Cafés

Cafés can be found in many of the city's art galleries. **ATENEUM** (Kaivokatu 2/+358.9.1733.6231) with its high-ceilinged classic charm, and **KIASMA** (Mannerheiminaukio 2/+358.9.1733.6504) with its cutting-edge modern design are aesthetically pleasing spots offering a good selection of café food. Kiasma also has a special kid's café, with pint-size tables and chairs for little people.

Any place marked *kahvila* (café) no matter how small or modest, usually brews a decent cup of coffee.

If you're looking for something beyond glossy downtown Helsinki, head to the Kallio neighbourhood, about a ten-minute tram ride from the centre of town, for the city's more colourful cafés. Once a working-class neighbourhood, Kallio is home to artists, students, writers, journalists, and some of Helsinki's more down-and-out denizens.

Creative lefties hang out at smokey **RYTMI** (Toinen Linja 2/ +358.9.7231.5550), just up from the Hakaniemi metro station. Rytmi also has a smoke-free room, and live music some evenings. The gruff-looking staff behind the counter are quite friendly if you manage to strike up a conversation. At the nearby Hakaniemi Market Hall, there are two down-home cafés, one with a large seating area on the second floor, and a smaller to-go food bar on the first floor.

KAHVILA TAIKALAMPPU (Torkkelinkatu 21/+358.9.773.4242) is like sitting in your eccentric aunt's living room, replete with brightly coloured mismatched tables and chairs. The proprietor knits in between taking orders and baking homemade *pulla*. Open until 7 pm every night.

Grand Old Dames Confectioner and pastry house **FAZER** has several locations around town including its flagship café and restaurant at **Kluuvikatu 3 (+358.9.6159.2959)**. A venerable Helsinki institution, this is where ladies who lunch lunch.

While you'll also find Fazer confectioneries and pastries in stores around town, this location stocks one of the largest selections of their melt-in-your-mouth chocolate, which rivals any made by the Swiss. Actually, founder Karl Fazer, who opened his first shop in Helsinki in 1891 in this very spot, came from Switzerland. *Fazerin sininen,* the milk chocolate in the blue wrapper, is the classic Finnish favourite. There's also a good selection of ice cream here.

The restaurant's dome-like back room creates an echo which means that you can hear interesting tidbits — provided you understand the language being spoken — from across the room.

In the 1930s and '40s, during the Golden Age of Finnish Film, many Finnish film stars including the legendary Regina Linnanheimo (1915–1995), who appeared in some 35 films during her career and won a Jussi (a Finnish Oscar), frequented Fazer as the movie studios of the day were nearby.

Reminiscent of a Viennese café, **CAFÉ EKBERG (Bulevardi 9/+358.9.6811.8660)** retains an old world charm from a time when Helsinki was largely a Swedish-speaking town. It's the place to go for mouth-watering cakes.

By the Seaside Experience an invigorating cuppa by visiting the outdoor Market Square (Kauppatori), which is just at the end of the Esplanade on the Helsinki harbourfront. (The Hakaniemi Market Square offers the same fare at less touristy prices.) In the orange-tented stands you can have a good strong coffee with *a munkkipossu* (literally "donut pig"), a sugar-coated donut with a jam filling. For something savoury, try one of the greasy meat pasties *(lihapiirakka)* or some salted fish. Fresh fruit and vegetables are also for sale. Provided you don't buy too much from the stalls selling touristy knick knacks, this genuine taste of Finland — there are market squares in every city throughout the country — will only set you back a couple of euros. Check out the larger-than-life Viking line cruise ships docked in the harbour that ply the waters between Stockholm and Helsinki. An added bonus is the lively bustle of market goers, sellers hawking their wares, and the occasional accordion player or musician competing with the hollering fishermen selling fresh fish from their boats.

> ## Try a *munkkipossu* – literally a "donut pig."

Further south along the boardwalk that circles the Helsinki waterfront are several kiosks and cafés including **CAFÉ URSULA** (Ehrenströmintie 3/+358.9.652.817), which is perched on the edge of Kaivopuisto Park and attracts an international crowd with its sublime view of the sea. Nearby, **CAFÉ CARUSEL** (Merisatamanranta 10/+358.9.622.4522), one of the few local cafés offering free coffee refills, also has a splendid sea panorama.

On the other side of Helsinki, **TAMMINIEMENTIEN KAHVILA** (Tamminiementie 8/+358.9.481.003) is housed in a gracious old antique-filled villa. Not renowned for its perky service, its warm décor, homemade pastries and fresh *pulla* more than make up for it. The café is near several museums and galleries, including the Helsinki City Art Museum Meilahti and the Urho Kekkonen Museum.

3.

Eating Out

Dining Out A foodie's delight, Helsinki has a variety of restaurants serving international cuisine — from Finnish to Thai — in just about every budget range.

With the exception of Sundays, when many restaurants are closed, most dinner restaurants are open until 11 or 12 pm. In general, breakfast is served between 7 and 10, lunch between 11 and 2 or 3 pm, and dinner from 4 until 10 or 11 pm.

Compared with Southern Europeans, Finns tend to eat lunch and dinner early. On weekdays, they often have their main meal midday, and eat something lighter at night, though this tradition is changing.

Tax and tip are included in the price, however, an extra tip will not be turned away. It's always a good idea to make a reservation to ensure that you get a table, especially at weekends, but if you're prepared to check out a few spots and see what's available, you can gamble on finding something at short notice. Many a restaurant *(ravintola)* around town feature the Helsinki Menu, which uses the season's best domestic ingredients prepared in the restaurant's own culinary style.

info

Finnish Food Although some traditional dishes call for liberal doses of cream or fat (some grandmas still serve meatballs with fat sauce), the Finnish diet is relatively healthy these days. Not known for being spicy, Finnish cuisine uses fresh ingredients such as fish, vegetables and berries, emphasising the natural flavours of the food.

Fish — raw, steamed, baked, fried, salted, or cured — is one of the staples of the diet; much of the fresh supply comes from the Baltic. Sausage and meat are abundant, while reindeer is a Finnish delicacy. Soups are popular, and potatoes or rice and salad almost always accompany meals. Salads feature the usual North American fare such as lettuce, tomatoes, and cucumbers, but also add distinctive fixings such as cabbage and beets.

Bread, served with most meals, is another basic. Typical Finnish bread is a dark rye, eaten with cheese – Finnish cheeses such as Lappi and Emmental are exported around the world – meat, or fish. Berries

(lingonberry and cranberry) and fruit are often incorporated into desserts, and cloudberries are a Finnish specialty from Lapland. *Rahka,* pudding made of milk or sour cream, and *kiisseli,* a berry soup, are abundant.

The tradition of pea soup and pancakes on Thursdays comes from an old army custom: Thick pea soup with or without ham stands as the main course; dessert is a pancake topped with a dollop of jam.

Crayfish season in August starts up a round of crayfish parties. The pricey crustacean is washed down with schnapps, preferably Finnish Koskenkorva; having a crayfish party hangover the next day is a national badge of honour.

Traditional Finnish cuisine draws its influences from Swedish and Russian cuisine. These days there's some very interesting fusion cuisine available in Helsinki, from Nordic-Asian to Fenno-French. Sample some reindeer pizza or Arctic char ravioli.

Vegetarian is not exactly the city's culinary calling card, however, most restaurants have decent meat-free options, and there are a few good veggie restaurants around.

Artsy Restaurants

KOSMOS (Kalevankatu 3/+358.9.647.255) is an august Helsinki institution and one of the best places to go for an excellent meal and to watch the city's movers and shakers — from the literati to businesspeople and ambassadors — in action.

Established in 1924, on what was then called Vladimir Street, Kosmos has been operated by the same family in the same spot since then. Katri Hepolampi, whose father was the founder, runs the dining room today and is herself a veritable character.

Kosmos serves "Helsinki cuisine," a long-standing mix of Russian, French, and Swedish influences combined with indigenous Finnish ingredients. Their weekday lunch menu offers delicacies such as Baltic herring, blinis with whitefish roe, sweetbread salad, and reindeer with spruce-shoot sauce.

The dining room has retained much of its original appearance, as created by then-architecture student Alvar Aalto, and furniture designers Einari Kyöstilä and Eino Räsänen, who carved the Hellenic motifs of the booth panels. Some of the more current clientele's work is on display, including pop-media artist Alvar Gullichsen's "Kosmo" and Juhani Harri's "Snow Queen." Stefan Lindfors, an international poster boy for Finnish design, remodelled the vestibule in 1993.

A ten-minute walk away is **TORI** (Punavuorenkatu 2/ +358.9.6874.3790), one of the hottest spots in town for the Helsinki who's who, frequented by a trend-conscious media crowd. Among Tori regulars are designer Stefan

Lindfors, who moved back to Helsinki a few years ago after a stretch in New York, Ville Valo, frontman for rock band HIM, and Maria Guzenina, former MTV Europe VJ and local media personality.

Tori serves Finnish international cuisine, including the city's best meatballs and mashed potatoes. Mains are in the 9 to 16 euro range, lunch 6 to 8 euros. Tori, which means "square," as in market square, doesn't accept reservations. Its 40-seat outdoor summer patio looks out onto Punavuori, a super-cool neighbourhood which is home to nifty boutiques and studios including that of Moon TV, a cheeky 24-hour cable lifestyle channel.

Some blocks away is a decidedly less style-conscious eatery. If you want good value for your money, heaps of basic Finnish food, and a Kaurismäki film-hued dining experience, try **RAVINTOLA VPK** (Albertinkatu 29/ +358.9.693.1581). Founded in 1945, the restaurant is run by the Voluntary Fire Brigade of Helsinki *(Helsingin vapaaehtoinen palokunta)* and serves a standard homestyle lunch with a choice of two warm mains — usually one meat and one fish — soup, rice and potatoes, a salad bar, bread, and dessert, all for less than 8 euros. Indeed, VPK's slogan is *"Perinteistä ruokaa ilman turhia trendikotkotuksia"* which roughly translates to "traditional food without useless trendy nonsense."

Complete with dark-vested waiters and melancholy music, the restaurant has an immaculate '50s style interior with trophy cases lining one wall and framed portraits lining another.

The lunch restaurant — it's only open from 11 to 3 pm — is in the inner courtyard; follow the signs from the street and hang a right.

Bohemian Rhapsodies Another boho gathering spot is **SEA-HORSE** (Kapteeninkatu 11/+358.9.628.169), a smokey place where locals meet for a drink or a meal. Poet Pablo Neruda, musician Dizzy Gillespie, and writer Jean Paul Sartre have graced the premises; Sartre is said to have liked it so much that he didn't want to leave. The food is hearty and filling: Crisp fried herring, meatballs, and *pyttipannu* (Scandinavian hash), a Finnish pan-fried specialty of potatoes, sausages, eggs, and onions. Traditional pea soup is served on Thursdays.

ELITE (Eteläinen Hesperiankatu 22/+358.9.434.2200), with its Left Bank atmosphere, has long been a haunt of artists, writers, and other creative types. Opened in 1932, the restaurant and bar in the Töölö neighbourhood, a five-minute tram ride from downtown, has a sprawling outdoor summer patio. One of the most popular entrées, the Tauno Palo steak with onion cream sauce, is named after a restaurant regular, the macho Finnish actor and film star Tauno Palo (1908–1982), who played more than 400 stage roles and acted in more than 60 films.

Locals Still in Töölö, several blocks away, a plaque marks the spot where novelist Salman Rushdie drank his first whiskey without security at **MESSENIUS** (Messeniuksenkatu 7/+358.9.241.4950), an unassuming neighbourhood restau-

Helsinki is reputed to have the best Russian restaurants.

rant with fish and meat mains, and a selection of beers. Not far from the Sibelius monument in Töölö, **LEHTOVAARA (Mechelininkatu 39/+358.9.440.833)**, established before independence, offers upscale dining with the priciest entrée — bear — at 50 euros.

On the other side of Töölönlahti, **JUTTUTUPA (Säästöpankinranta 6/ +358.9.774.48.60)**, another of Helsinki's older restaurants, established in 1908 in a grand Jugend-style building, offers traditional Finnish cuisine, from salmon soup to grilled lamb, duck, and reindeer. Verdaces, a popular fish dish, goes for just under 10 euros.

SALVE (Hietalahdenranta 11/+358.9.603.455), founded in 1897, is decidedly more down-home with its skipper-themed interior and fried herring and mash menu that boasts large servings and listings in seven different languages including Spanish. From here you can see the Kvaerner Masa shipyards, where many of the massive cruise ships that ply the oceans of the world are built.

Visit **LAPPI (Annankatu 22/+358.9.645.550)** for a taste of Lapland, replete with numerous reindeer options. **KELLA-RIKROUVI (Pohjoinen Makasiinikatu 6/+358.9.686.0730)** is the city's only genuine cellar restaurant. Cosy, and in the mid-price range, Kellarikrouvi serves up traditional Finnish cuisine in a building that was designed by the famous architectural trio of Eliel Saarinen, Armas Lindgren, and Herman Gesellius.

Russian

Helsinki is reputed to have the best Russian restaurants in the Nordic region, a curious feature of the city, as many were established long before the recent influx of Russians. Blinis (a buckwheat pancake served with sour cream and roe) are sure to please and bear is big. In fact, blinis are so popular that in January and February many Helsinki restaurants host special blini weeks.

ŠAŠLIK (Neitsytpolku 12/+358.9.7425.5500) is worth going to for the tsarist décor alone. The two main dining rooms are lavish, but the seven private rooms of varying sizes, each decorated in a different theme, are spectacular. The à la carte menu includes a diverse selection of Russian cuisine, including of course blinis and bear. Russian wine is served, and Russian troubadours play music nightly.

ALEXANDER NEVSKI (Pohjoisesplanadi 17/+358.9.686.9560) evokes a traditional Russian manor with its heavy draperies, glistening samovars, and crisp linen tablecloths. Dinner with wine and dessert is about 50 to 60 euros per person.

Helsinki's oldest Russian restaurant, BELLEVUE (Rahapajankatu 3/+358.9.179.560), is in Katajanokka, just on the other side of the impressive Uspensky Cathedral; its plush modern interior belies its age (it's been around since 1917) and recreates a sense of tsarist times, complete with Russian music.

Cosy BABUSHKA IRA (Uudenmaankatu 28/+358.9.680.1405)

— the red damask curtains and paintings are from St. Petersburg — recalls grandma's cooking, while traditional **KASAKKA** (Meritullinkatu 13/+358.9.6129.2720) features Russian-speaking staff. Kasakka's grilled spiced steak is about 20 euros. Equally charming, food and interior-wise, **HARITON** (Kasarmikatu 44/+358.9.622.1717) and **TROIKKA** (Caloniuksenkatu 3/+358.9.445.229) are less pricey than Šašlik, Nevski, and Bellevue.

Cosmopolitan **MAXILL** (Korkeavuorenkatu 4/+358.638.873) bar and restaurant is popular with style-hounds and power-brokers for its cosmopolitan fare and striking red and black interior. A few doors down, **SOFRA LONDON** (Korkeavuorenkatu 2A/+358.9.622.26.25) offers modern Turkish and Middle Eastern cuisine in a swish setting.

G.W. SUNDMANS (Eteläranta 16/+358.9.622.6410), on the shore of the harbour in a house originally built for sea captain Sundman, is the only restaurant in town other than Chez Dominique to hold a Michelin star. Sundmans boasts an excellent wine cellar; fillet of deer with pepper game sauce clocks in at under 35 euros.

For a New York moment, try **TONY'S DELI** (Bulevardi 2/+358.9.6129.4913) with its Manhattan-like élan. **PAPA GIOVANNI** (Keskuskatu 7/+358.9.622.6010) in Helsinki's World Trade Centre is a taste of Little Italy, and **BELGE BAR AND BISTRO** (Kluuvikatu 5/+358.9.622.9620) serves Belgian beer, mussels, and frites. **KYNSILAUKKA RAVINTOLA GARLIC** (Fredikinkatu 22/+358.9.651.939) offers an entire menu of food and drinks infused with liberal doses of garlic. Garlic martini, anyone?

Ethnic Eats Multi-level EATZ (Mikonkatu 15/+358.9.687.7240) offers up several restaurants in one with eight different menus including Thai, Tex-Mex, Indian, and Japanese, which is served on the first-level sushi bar belt. Co-owned by Sakke Järvenpää, who heads the Leningrad Cowboys (self-proclaimed as the world's worst rock band and immortalised in the Kaurismäki films), and Formula One race car driver Mika Salo, Eatz has one of the city's largest summer patios — 400 seats. Järvenpää designed Eatz's whimsical interior.

Many consider NAMASKAAR (Mannerheimintie 100/ +358.9.477.1960) to be the best Indian restaurant in town with its all-you-can eat evening buffet for 15 to 18 euros, which is available only at the Mannerheimintie location. There are several 'Skaar locations in town including Namaskaar **WOK IT** in Sanomatalo, **RAVINTOLA NAMASKAAR** (Bulevardi 6A/+358.9.622.011.55), and **NAMASKAAR EXPRESS** (Aleksanterinkatu 36B/+358.9.278.1363).

Across from department store Stockmann, **YADE WOK AND BAR** (Keskuskatu 3/+358.9.6124.5759) doubles as a restaurant and club, with Thai, Japanese, and Vietnamese cuisine on ground level. Noodles, ramen, and salads make for a quick meal, while the club downstairs plays top 40 and R 'n' B.

SATKAR (Lönnrotinkatu 26/+358.9.611.077), with its speedy service and good lunch deals, is one of the best Nepalese restos in town while **MAITHAI** (Annankatu 31-33/+358.9.685.6850) serves up — you guessed it — Thai food, with several vegetarian dishes on the menu, and Thai beer. **ANTIOKIA ATABAR** (Eerinkinkatu 44B/+358.9.6940.367) dishes up Turkish food to the accompaniment of belly dancing, and chic **FA-ROUGE** (Yrjönkatu 6/+358.9.612.3455) is Helsinki's only Lebanese restaurant.

Sushi Time   The Japanese and the Finnish share a love of raw fish, and the popularity of Asian cuisine has grown here in recent years. Owned and operated by Yoshio Tamura, **GYOSAI-SUSHI BAR** (Runeberginkatu 40B/+358.9.241.3440) is officially the city's smallest restaurant, with five seats, while **NORISUSHI BAR** in the Old Market Hall (Eteläranta 1/+358.9.260.0027) makes great sushi in slightly more spacious environs. At **SUSHI BAR ICHIBAN** (Mikonkatu 8/

+358.9.672.345), tucked away on the second floor, you can get a full meal deal with sushi, miso soup, and tea for under 10 euros. When Japan's Prince and Princess Hitachi visited town, the Japanese embassy ordered dinner from **KABUKI** (Lapinlahdenkatu 12/+358.9.694.9446), run by Yoshiaki Takayama, and known as a place where local celebs host parties.

French Dressing

Booking is a must for **CHEZ DOMINIQUE** (Ludviginkatu 3–5/+358.9.612.7393), holder of two coveted Michelin stars, as the chi-chi restaurant usually has a weeklong waiting list. Scandinavian gourmet with a French attitude, Chez Dominique is run by celebrity chef Hans Välimäki and his young 20- and 30-something crew. **LA PETITE MAISON** (Huvilakatu 28A/+358.9.260.9680) in upscale Eira offers French cuisine at reasonable prices with an excellent selection of wines. Thirty-five-year-old **RAVINTOLA LYON** (Mannerheimintie 56/+358.9.408.131), opposite the Opera House, combines quality Finnish ingredients with French culinary know-how in a warm Lyon-like milieu. Their Helsinki menu is 46 euros, the French menu 62, and the vegetarian 38.

Late Night

Although many fast food places keep late hours (see Cheap Eats), one of the few restaurants whose kitchen is open very late — until 3:30 am seven days a week — is **MANALA** (Dagmarinkatu 2/+358.9.580.77707), just behind the Parliament Buildings in the Botta nightclub complex. Although Manala means "hell" in Finnish, the eatery, which doubles as a disco, is no such place. It serves up tasty Finnish and international favourites, including spaghetti bolognese and vegetarian pizza, into the wee hours of the morning.

Vegetarian While not necessarily Helsinki's culinary specialty, good vegetarian cuisine can be found. Many restaurants, from fast-food chain Hesburger to Thai restaurant Maithai, have decent meat-free options. For strictly veg, try **SILVOPLEE** (Toinen linja 3/+358.9.726.0900), run by actress Satu Silvo, who serves a living food buffet. Juices, salads, soups, Finnish cakes, and shortbreads are all prepared organically. Well worth the money, Silvoplee is nevertheless pricey.

HERNE AND NAURIS (Munkkisaarenkatu 16/+358.9.850.11.858), run by the Helsinki Deaconess Institute, organises poetry readings, jazz, rock 'n' roll, and theatre to accompany its reasonably priced fare. Much-lauded **ZUCCHINI VEGETARIAN CAFÉ** (Fabianinkatu 4/+358.9.622.2907) is right downtown, and features an ever-changing menu with generous portions.

Splashing Out

Finland's Frank Lloyd Wright, architect Alvar Aalto, and his first wife Aino designed the interior of **SAVOY** (Eteläesplanadi 14/+358.9.176.571) right down to each table's wavy Aalto vase, which was initially called the Savoy Vase. The eighth-floor restaurant looks so contemporary that it's hard to believe it was designed almost 70 years ago, in 1937. From the dining room and the adjacent terrace, there's a fabulous city panorama from Uspensky Cathedral to Stockmann's.

Finnish and international specialities are on the menu including *vorschmack* and Marski's shot, two favourites of Savoy's most famous regular, marshal Mannerheim, Finland's wartime leader and president from 1944 to 1946. Marski's shots are made with vodka, aquavit, dry vermouth and gin, stirred together and served ice cold. *Vorschmack* is an hors d'oeuvre of herring, garlic, onions, and lamb cooked in butter over a low flame. According to legend, the well-travelled Mannerheim introduced *vorschmack* to Finland. Savoy's menu features fish, reindeer, and meat; dinner for two with a good wine will set you back about 150 euros.

Other high-end eateries include top notch **RESTAURANT GEORGE** (Kalevankatu 17/+358.9.647.662), known for its Menu George, a set menu at 75 euros that includes duck breast carpaccio, deer seasoned with garlic bread and thyme sauce, a cheese plate, and gooseberry white chocolate pannacotta with vanilla ice cream. Considered by many to be the city's top fish and seafood restaurant, **HAVIS AMANDA** (Pohjoisesplanadi 17/+358.9.6869.5660) is just across from the harbourfront Havis Amanda statue, which is also called The Daughter of the Baltic and is regarded as a symbol of Helsinki.

PALACE GOURMET (Eteläranta 10/+358.9.1345.6715) offers a harbour view and a seven-course tasting menu, while **NOKKA** (Kanavaranta 7/+358.9.687.7330), in a gorgeously renovated warehouse, won the award for the city's best Helsinki Menu in 2002.

Opened in 1867, glass-fronted **KAPPELI** (Eteläesplanadi 1/+358.9.681.244) looks out over the Esplanade Park. The restaurant, bar, and café was one of the hangouts of composer Jean Sibelius; artist Akseli Gallen-Kallela, who designed the Finnish Pavilion for the Paris World Expo in 1900 and illustrated the Finnish national epic, the *Kalevala;* and writer and poet Eino Leino (1878–1926), whose former table is still in the Sali side.

Architect and interior designer Kaisa Blomstedt tastefully revamped the fancy Kappeli restaurant, while the cellar bar was redone and jazzed up by Leningrad Cowboy Sakke Järvenpää, who has styled many groovy interiors around town.

Celebrity Watch Fine dining is also available across the street at **KÄMP RESTAURANT (Pohjoisesplanadi 29/ +358.9.576.111)**, which specialises in high-end international cuisine. The restaurant is located in Helsinki's only five-star hotel, which was established in 1887, and recently extensively restored to its opulent original. The ritzy hotel has a long history of hosting international and Finnish greats including composer Jean Sibelius, artist Akseli Gallen-Kallela, and poet Eino Leino, whose legendary parties often lasted for several days.

An often-told story is that of Sibelius's response to his wife's query as to when he'd return home from one of the never-ending soirées: "I'm a composer, not a clairvoyant."

Marshal Mannerheim had his own suite, which these days is one of the hotel's most sought-after (and luxurious) suites and has hosted celebrities such as pop diva Whitney Houston, who liked it so much that she stayed for an additional week.

Other famous guests, largely rock and pop stars, have included Elton John, Cher, the Red Hot Chili Peppers, Sting, Tom Jones, Tina Turner, The Smashing Pumpkins, Savage Garden, AC/DC, Bryan Ferry, Marilyn Manson, Depeche Mode, Roxette, Shakira, and media baron Rupert Murdoch. The lobby level Kämp Bar is a good place for celeb spotting.

Island Eats Numerous islands — there are 315 — dot the Helsinki harbour. Therein lie several good restaurants

not a clairvoyant."

JEAN SIBELIUS

and cafés, many of which operate only during the summer season that runs from early May to late September.

From the main harbour, you can see **NJK (Valkosaari/ +358.9.639.261)**, popular for crayfish parties, and **KLIPPAN (Luoto/+358.9.633.408)**. Both are housed in elegant villas on separate islands and the view from each island is worth the five-minute boat ride. At NJK, mains are in the 20 to 30 euro range, with dishes such as braised turbot with beurre blanc sauce and some spicier ones. Klippan's boat departs from the Ullanlinna jetty, while NJK's leaves from a pier just south of Silja Line's Olympic Terminal.

SÄRKÄNLINNA (+358.9.1345.6756) on Särkkä Island — the island and its fortress are listed as a UNESCO cultural heritage site — features a signature dish of warm, smoked salmon with creamed morels and new potatoes for just under 30 euros. Another house speciality is tar-flavoured crème brûlée. The island's boat departs from a pier near Café Ursula.

Southwest of Kaivopuisto Park, the nautical ambience of **HSS RESTAURANT (Liuskasaari/+358.9.2709.7040)** was one of the locations for *Crime and Punishment,* an early film by Aki Kaurismäki based on the Dostoyevsky novel of the same name. Finnish dishes and a few continental European favourites are on the menu, as well as a large selection of fish including roe, whitefish, pike, and fried Baltic herring served with mashed potatoes. Boats to HSS depart from the southern end of Kapteeninkatu in Eira.

Summer restaurant **SAARI** ("island" in Finnish) is on Sirpalesaari (+358.9.7425.5566) and serves fusion food and Finnish delicacies from reindeer to salmon. The escargot au gratin is inspired by French cuisine; other specialties include bear, as the restaurant is run by the owners of Russian restaurant Šašlik. Boat transportation runs from the pier behind Café Carusel on Merisatamanranta.

UUNISAARI RESTAURANT AND CAFÉ on Uunisaari (+358.9.636.870), just off Kaivopuisto, is open year round and offers slightly more casual dining in a pizza patio atmosphere.

Cheap Fast Eats

Many cafés and restaurants offer sandwiches, salads, soups, and basic lunch entrées for less than 10 euros. If you're looking for a quick and inexpensive meal, such as kebabs, burgers, pizza, check out the following spots.

NEW BAMBOO CENTER (Annankatu 29/+358.9.694.3117) sounds like a furniture store, but it's a Chinese Malaysian restaurant with speedy service. The décor — pale green walls — and the food are just like what you'd expect to get in New York's Chinatown. The best feature? Aside from the ample portions that you can spice up or down according to your preference, the Asian staff speaks rapid-fire Finnish, so fast that even natives can't always catch what they're saying. Six to 10 euros for plentiful portions; the place is packed at lunch, but it's easier to snag a table in the evening.

WRONG NOODLE BAR (Vuorikatu 14/+358.611.500), in Kaisaniemi's Fennia shopping centre, is a Tokyo-style noodle bar with a designer quirk: the Calvin Klein T-shirts are for sale, the CK watches are not. Right next to the Kinopalatsi movieplex, Wrong's serves up a good selection of noodles. There's another **WRONG** at Annankatu 21 (+358.9.2486.2442).

Maybe a modicum healthier than McDonald's, **HESBURGER** (Aleksanterinkatu 13/+358.9.2709.0030) is a domestic fast food chain with a Finnish twist. Try the hamburger served on the heavy dark rye that's so popular here — *reissumies* bread. Vegetarians swear by the veggie burgers; there are several Hesburger locations around town.

There are many good pizzerias in the city, but if you're looking to satisfy an all-you-can-eat appetite, head for **GOLDEN RAX PIZZA BUFFET**, which has several locations, including Mikonkatu 8 (+358.9.478.00555) and the Forum shopping complex. Their pizza, wings, pasta, salad, and beverage buffet for 7 euros and change is guaranteed to leave you feeling sated.

Voted the city's best kebabery, **STADIN KEBAB** (*stadi* is slang for "city") stays open until 5 am (Eerikinkatu 14/ +358.9.622.4791 and other locations) and offers fast and filling kebabs in the 5 euro range.

The grill kiosk (*grillikioski*) is a special late night tradition — they are only open at night — best enjoyed in the wee drunken hours. Serving hotdogs, meat pasties, hamburgers, and fries (all to-go for a couple of euros), numerous grills dot the city. According to Helsinki's hip barometer, *City* magazine (which publishes two English-language editions a year), the best one is in Töölö at the corner of Runeberginkatu and Sandelsinkatu. Töölön tori-grilli, open till 5 am every morning, has close to 20 different hamburger options and gives taxi drivers free coffee.

4.

Bars, Nightclubs, and Live Music

Drinking   A few words about Finnish booze and drinking culture: Finns drink — a lot.

Once-restrictive alcohol laws have influenced drinking customs. Add to that traditionally high alcohol prices, and an all-or-nothing attitude — i.e., if we're going to drink, let's do it properly — and it seems that drinking is a national sport and a sort of social release. Sober, many Finns tend to be reserved, but after a few drinks they open up and become rather talkative. This may sound like a stereotype, but in many cases it holds true.

In recent years, drinking habits have become more moderate. As a nation, Finns are not statistically among the world's top drinkers, though you'd never guess this if you were out on a Thursday, Friday, or Saturday night in Helsinki. It's not surprising that many a foreigner has misunderstood the Finnish word for "cheers," *kippis*, to mean "get pissed."

DRINKS

Beer and Cider There are several brands of "Finnish" beer including Karhu, Lapin Kulta, Koff — though all are now owned by international brewing conglomerates. Technically, Olvi is the only remaining wholly Finnish-owned brewery.

Beers with low alcohol content can be purchased in grocery stores, as can mild ciders. Stronger beers, those with alcohol content greater than 5 per cent, are available in bars and restaurants, or from one of the liquor stores operated by the fittingly named state monopoly, Alko.

Sahti is a traditional Finnish beer brewed using ancient methods, and in recent years it has gained a worldwide following. One of its better-known fans is international beer guru Michael Jackson. Perry (pear cider) is popular, as is apple cider; both domestic and British brands are available. Gin Long Drink, known as *lonkero,* a mix of gin and grape soda, is a Finnish cooler that's been around since the '50s.

Wine and Spirits To be perfectly frank, most Finnish wines can't compete with French, Italian, or Australian wines. If hard liquor is your thing, Finlandia vodka is widely available straight, martinied, or cocktailed. Or shaken but not stirred. In the latest James Bond flick, *Die Another Day,* Agent 007 has switched from Absolut to Finlandia. Given the healthy rivalry that exists between the Finns and Swedes, this is a bit of a Finnish coup — even though Finlandia's majority ownership is actually American.

Koskenkorva is the quintessential Finnish vodka,

which is used to spike up just about any beverage and features in numerous drinks including the perennial favourite, *salmiakkikossu,* a mixture of salted liquorice candy and vodka. Definitely an acquired taste, the thick, sweet and salty black drink is served in shots. Another sugary domestic favourite is the silver toffee shot, made with toffee and hard liquor.

Drinking is a national sport.

Koskenkorva *(kossu)* is so integral to Finnish culture that when the state-owned company that makes Koskenkorva was to be sold off some years ago, a number of academics, artists, and MPs formed a Pro Koskenkorva Movement to battle the trend of globalisation. (They won.)

Going Out As for an evening dress code, just about anything goes these days, though chic Euro casual is your best bet. For some nightclubs and restaurants people really dress up.

Diehard barflys and nightclubbers won't be disappointed with Helsinki's many offerings. Be forewarned, there are a few places where the age limit is 18, but for most night spots it's 20, and for many nightclubs it's 23 or 24. And doormen do ask for ID, even if you're well over the minimum age.

Cover charges vary. Many pubs and bars don't have covers, unless there's a band playing. Most nightclubs do have a cover after 9 or 10 pm, ranging from a couple of euros up to 10 euros. There's often a mandatory coat check, particularly in the winter, which costs 1 or 2 euros.

Bars and Clubs Uudenmaankatu and its environs hold court as the trendy drinking (and shopping) district. Conveniently there are several bars therein, so if one isn't to your fancy, you can easily move on to another.

BAR 9 (Uudenmaankatu 9/+358.9.621.4055), known as a media hangout, draws an intellectual crew of poets, architects, designers, and other creative media types. A few doors down, **TAPASTA** (Uudenmaankatu 13/+358.9.640.724), also frequented by the artsy set, has good tapas and designer beers.

Soda, formerly one of the street's biggest draws, at the corner of Annankatu and Uudenmaankatu, has been replaced by a Finnhits karaoke bar, owned by one of the ex-wives of former Olympic ski jumper Matti Nykänen.

Down the street and around the corner is smokey **EROTTAJA BAR** (Erottajankatu 15-17/+358.9.611.196), and über-hip **KERMA** (Erottajankatu 7/+358.9.680.2655), which features an all-day bar downstairs, dining, and music by top-notch DJs from home and abroad upstairs. DJ Jori Hulkkonen (a.k.a Zyntherius) and DJ collective NuSpirit Helsinki are among Kerma's illustrious international disc-spinning alumnae.

A Bit of Soho **TEATTERI** (Pohjoisesplanadi 2/+358.9.681.1130), designed by Briton Rupert Gardner, epitomises Helsinki's change from European outpost to style central. Twenty years ago Teatteri was a nightclub called Hot Lips that, as an *Observer* journalist put it, "attracted the sort of eastern European men who talk 'beezneez' while groping bottle-blonde Estonian hookers." Then, for several years, it was a pub restaurant called Happy Days, where you could enjoy an overpriced burger in a not-so-happy setting. Walk in today and you could be in London, New York, or Hong Kong.

The lounge bar is airy and spacious, and the international jetset tumbles in for a drink, partly because of its central location at the end of the Esplanade Park. The lofty restaurant, with its white gauzy curtains and sleek design, serves good Finnish-continental cuisine.

The upstairs Teatteri Klubi disco is chic and cheesy at the same time, with well-dressed, happily drunk Finns and the occasional celebrity dancing the night away to top 40 hits. VIP lounge members include Formula One race car driver Mika Häkkinen, and many of the city's beautiful people.

Sauna Bars

Possibly the best-known Finnish export before Nokia came along, the sauna is social, cultural, and healthy, and not usually taken in mixed company. Historically, saunas have been regarded as pure, clean places, where physical and spiritual cleansing took place.

A unique element of Helsinki nightlife is the sauna bar. At CAFÉ TIN TIN TANGO (Töölöntorinkatu 7/ +358.9.270.90972), in the trendy neighbourhood of Töölö, you can book the café's back sauna for a Saturday night sauna with the gang for 17 euros and up.

Tin Tin Tango has a mini laundromat, music by DJs on weekend nights, and serves an all-day breakfast — something of a rarity in Helsinki — until 1 am daily. A neighbourhood fave, Tin Tin has a loyal, local clientele including actors and actresses, hockey players, and other athletes such as 20-something javelin thrower Harri Haatainen, a regular on the Helsinki night scene.

Downtown, **SAUNABAR** (Eerikinkatu 27/+358.9.586.5550) is a popular spot for a sauna, playing pool, and listening to some tunes. Saturday night's long-running "License to Chill" DJ'd sessions are well loved, as are Saunabar's playful dressing rooms equipped with aquariums. Through the courtyard of number 27, around the corner and down the stairs, the bar's two saunas (segregated by sex) are open to all on Sundays and Mondays but must be booked in advance on other days.

To Moscow with Love Owned by the filmmaking Kaurismäki brothers, Aki and Mika, **Москва (Eerikinkatu 11/+358.9.611.200)** and **Corona**, next door (+358.9.642.002), are part of the Andorra movie theatre building, which screens good indie films.

Mockba, decorated in Russian kitsch, is a small bar with an ironic '50s Soviet attitude. In the corner, a record player cranks out Russian tunes. On the wall, a picture of the late Matti Pellonpää, a much-loved actor in the Kaurismäki films.

Corona, with its numerous pool and billiard tables, is more Milan than Moscow. Cinephiles meet here before going to watch films at Andorra, and if you're lucky you might see one of the owners, whose quirky films about life's underdogs have inspired a cult-like following worldwide. People of all ages hang out at Corona and at Mockba (pronounced "Moskva," the name of the bar uses the Cyrillic spelling of the Russian word for Moscow).

On the next block, **MOTHER** (Eerikinkatu 2/+358.9.612.1012), designed by the ubiquitous Stefan Lindfors, is a slick lounge bar frequented by a young, trendy crowd.

Tractors and Karaoke
ZETOR (Kaivopiha/+358.9.666.966) is a little piece of the countryside in the heart of Helsinki. Tucked in the courtyard behind Vanha, the old university house, Zetor has a zany farm-style interior designed by Leningrad Cowboy Sakke Järvenpää, with tables built around old tractors for swilling back pints or eating a meal.

Neighbourhood karaoke bar **PATAÄSSÄ** (Mariankatu 9/ +358.9.626.076) in Kruununhaka is favoured by locals and domestic pop stars alike: Finnish chart-topper Paula Koivuniemi has been known to take over the mike here.

Pubs
There are numerous Irish and British pubs around town including **O'MALLEYS** and the **WILLIAM K** chain. English-style pub **SIR EINO** (Eteläesplanadi 18/+358.9.5420.0700) is

named after poet Eino Leino (1878–1926), who captured Finnish melancholy so well: "Short time's to us allotted till our urn," and was also the first Finnish translator of Dante. Spacious yet cosy, the after-work pub has a large selection of beers on tap from Kilkenny and Guinness to Finnish ales. Just across the street in the Esplanade Park, there's a statue commemorating Leino.

A large selection of Finnish and international beers is also available at **PAINOBAARI (Sanomatalo/+358.9.6812.140)**, which is in the same glassy building as Finland's largest daily newspaper, *Helsingin Sanomat*. Editorial staffers, among others, frequent Painobaari.

Former US president Bill Clinton is rumoured to have whistle-stopped at **VANHA (Mannerheimintie 3B/+358.9.13114.368)**, the grand, old university students' building, en route to Russia when he was a student. Vanha offers inexpensive drinks and eats.

Drinks with a View   Atop the 14-storey Torni Hotel, Helsinki's first "skyscraper," the **ATELJEE BAR (Kalevankatu 5/ +358.9.131.131)** offers one of the city's best views. On a clear day you can see all the way to Estonia.

Take the elevator to the 12th floor and then climb up the narrow spiral staircase to the tiny bar, which despite its size, always seems to have space for a few more.

Known as an artists' bar since the 1950s, partly because artists display their work in exchange for giving one painting to the hotel, Ateljee is frequented by everyone from locals to tourists and Eurocrats these days. (If you suffer from vertigo, Torni's ground-level American Bar with its cushy couches spells off Ateljee's dizzying heights.)

Torni's 12th-floor bathrooms boast a different view of the city with their floor-to-ceiling mirrored windows — a one-of-a-kind washroom experience, indeed. The ladies is better than the gents as it has a corner panorama.

Before the Second World War, the hotel's visitors included US president Herbert Hoover, Swedish prince Bertil, and well-known figures from the Finnish arts scene such as writers Mika Waltari, whose *Sinuhe the Egyptian* was widely translated in the 1940s and '50s, and F.E. Sillanpää, who received the Nobel Prize for literature in 1939 for his novel *Silja the Maid*.

At the end of the war in 1944, the Soviet authorities took over the hotel. When they left in 1947, the hotel was in such bad shape that Torni's insurance company wanted nothing to do with it. Fortunately, things turned around and the hotel was restored. Today, Torni is a good example of 1930s functionalism.

For a different view of the city, try the **PALACE HOTEL** (Eteläranta 10/+358.9.134.561) rooftop patio that looks out over the harbour. On a sunny day, you'll feel as though you're on the deck of a tall ship (steep drinks prices included) as you watch the boats in the harbour below.

Best Bubbly CAFÉ CARELIA (Mannerheimintie 56/+358.9.270.90.976), opposite the National Opera, focuses on Fenno-French cuisine, but one of its novelties is the extensive champagne selection (from Veuve to 1981 Krug), with some 20 to 25 different types of bubbly. Here, select champagnes can be ordered by the glass, something of a rarity in Helsinki. The pricing is quite reasonable, for example, a glass of Jacquesson et Fils Perfection Brut or Piper Hiedsieck Brut Cuvee 2000 is in the 7 euro range. This space was formerly an apothecary and some of the pharmacy's original décor remains.

Bar Tram Trams are unique to Helsinki; no other Finnish city has kept them. During the summer months, you can sightsee and sip beer at the same time by taking the red Pub Tram (Spårakoff) that picks up passengers in front of the Opera House, the Market Square, and on Mikonkatu.

Kallio Pub Crawl The Kallio neighbourhood, a 15-minute tram trip or a quick subway ride (get off at Sörnäinen station) from the Railway Station, is home to creative types (read: people with cool jobs that don't come with big salaries) owing to its affordable rents and abundance of studio apartments. Kallio hosts some of the city's liveliest and grittiest bars (happy hour starts at 9 am!), and a pint here will cost you considerably less than downtown.

Helsinkians, especially those who live in other parts of town, may warn you about Kallio, citing its dangers (such as drug dealing and prostitution). While there are a few rough areas with their string of sex bars and dodgy characters, compared with the truly scary areas of some big European, North American, and Asian cities, Kallio

73

is relatively benign. Regular professional folk live here — the president owns a Kallio apartment, which she lived in before taking office. Of late, the area has become trendy for its perceived down-and-out-ness.

ROSKAPANKKI (Helsinginkatu 20/+358.9.735.488) is a good ol' neighbourhood pub that draws people from other neighbourhoods. The corner jukebox plays Finnish and international hits, and a beer costs a couple of euros. Roskapankki means "garbage bank," a nod to the massive Finnish banking crisis that was underway when the pub opened ten years ago.

Just down the street and under the same ownership, **ILTAKOULU** (Vaasankatu 5/+358.9.711.611) also offers cheap drinks and a convivial atmosphere. Part of Iltakoulu's charm comes from the fact that *iltakoulu* means "night school" in Finnish; saying that you're off to night school sounds much better than saying you're off to the pub.

Kallio hosts some of the city's liveliest and grittiest bars.

In keeping with the trumped up educational theme, the pub's walls are lined with black and white portraits of former Finnish presidents. Check out the particularly sombre shot of "Ukko-Pekka" (Old Man Pete) Svinhufvud, who served as prime minister and president during the 1930s and before that, was instrumental in the battle that led to the country's independence. His Swedish surname literally translates to "Swinehead." Perhaps he looks so serious because before independence, he was banished to Siberia for three years.

Tucked away at the other end of Kallio is tiny **PUB SIRDIE** (Kolmas Linja 21/+358.694.2998), one of the filming locations for the Kaurismäki film *Calamari Union,* a dark comedy about a group of men who set off on a journey from working-class Kallio for the wealthy Eira neighbourhood. One of Helsinki's best jukeboxes is here, especially if you want to hear classic Finnish crooners such as Olavi Virta.

While **STELLA STAR CLUB** (Sturenkatu 27B/+358.9.58.400.061) is not technically in Kallio (it's in neighbouring Vallila), its camp '80s milieu has made it a fashionable spot where young movers and shakers host parties, and Finnish rock stars, supermodels, and former beauty queens mingle. A host of decent bands can be found on the bill.

Gay Bars Helsinki, and indeed Finland, is not quite as progressive as its Nordic neighbour Sweden, which was one of the first countries in the world to legalise same-sex marriage. In Finland, until the early '70s, it was illegal to engage in homosexual activity. Thankfully the climate is changing. SETA (+358.9.681.2580/www.seta.fi), the association for sexual equality, provides resources for gays and lesbians.

DTM (Iso Roobertinkatu 28/+358.9.676.315), short for Don't Tell Mama, is the biggest and best-known gay club in town, with a multi-floor disco and nightclub, a bar, and a café. DTM hosts fab drag shows, and on Saturday nights

75

the upstairs is for ladies only.

LOST & FOUND (Annankatu 6/+358.9.612.1882) is as popular with the het set as it is with the gay and lesbian crowd. **NALLE PUB** (Kaarlenkatu 3–5/+358.9.701.5543) is lesbian-friendly, and **ROOM** (Erottaja 5/+358.9.622.70.440) is one of the city's newer gay bars, aimed at a younger crowd.

An older crowd hangs out at **CON HOMBRES** (Eerikinkatu 14/+358.9.608.826), just opposite Corona, **HERCULES** (Lön-nrotinkatu 4/+358.9.612.1776), and **MANN'S STREET** (Mannerhei-mintie 12A 1/+358.9.612.1103), which has a disco, karaoke bar, and a regular bar that's open in the afternoons.

Nightlife For the most up-to-date info on parties, raves, gigs, dance clubs, concerts, and DJs, pick up the free glossy weekly leaflet called "Helsinki Clubland & Elokuvat," which provides movie and club listings, and is available

BARS, NIGHTCLUBS, AND LIVE MUSIC

in cafés, bars, restaurants, and cinemas around town.

Although the leaflet is in Finnish for the most part, much of the club info lists dates as numbers — 12.6 is the 12th of June, for example — and the names of bands and DJs are recognisable regardless of whether you understand Finnish or not.

Asking around in record shops, bars, and cafés is another good way of finding out about events that are not widely advertised but everyone in-the-know knows about.

Record shops **STUPIDO** (www.stupido.fi) and **STREET BEAT** (www.streetbeat.ac) have good websites that feature gig listings in English.

Nightclubbing

KAARLE XII (Kasarmikatu 40/+358.9.612.9990) or "Kalle," as it's known, named after a Swedish king, is a mainstream bar and disco in a grand old aristocratic building. Friday and Saturday nights are packed and there's usually a line-up to get in after 9 pm:ish. Wednesday and Thursday nights — the new Friday nights — draw big crowds. Lawyers, photographers, cosmeticians, techies, and artists (read: everybody) come here for dancing on the second-floor disco, which plays top 40 hits, or to sing in the Suomi bar downstairs, where they play only Finnish music.

KAIVOHUONE (Iso puistotie 1/+358.9.684.1530) first opened its doors back in 1838 and was originally a water spa. Located in Kaivopuisto park, just next to the exclusive Eira embassy area, the regal club is popular year round;

there's something scheduled just about every night of the week. Their summer patio is one of the city's busiest and attracts an all-ages crowd.

MANALA (Dagmarinkatu 2/+358.9.408.602) features several floors of dancing to music from live bands and the latest MTV tunes. Manala is part of Botta, which has been a Helsinki nightspot for more than 90 years.

Star Gazing

Movie star Keanu Reeves, pop diva Whitney Houston, and Rolling Stone Mick Jagger have all strutted their stuff at the venerable **HELSINKI CLUB** (Yliopistonkatu 8/+358.9.4332.6340), which has a minimum age of 24 and is open seven nights a week until 4 am. The nightclub is also popular with Finnish celebs, from race car drivers to models such as Janina Frostell, who penned the lyrics to a recent Eurovision song contest entry and was named one of the world's sexiest women by British lad magazine *Arena*.

Electronica pop star Moby visited **LADY MOON** (Kaivokatu 12/+358.9.6843.7370) nightclub when he was in town. Nearby, **10TH FLOOR** (Kaivokatu 3A/+358.9.1311.8223) is a nightclub/restaurant/bar that's atop the Sokos department store. With one of the best views of the city by night, 10th Floor has a reputation of being a meet-market for the 30-plus crowd.

Recently revamped **TIIKERI** (Yrjönkatu 36/+358.9.565.7800) is frequented by models (current and erstwhile), television types, and other mucky-mucks. Started by Sedu Koskinen, a fixture on the Helsinki scene, the exclusive club used to be called Tiger — *tiikeri* means "tiger" in Finnish. Around the corner, another of Koskinen's recent creations, **JAM JAM (Simonkatu 6/+358.9.586.0710)** is also a celeb-heavy night spot, with a restaurant in the back.

NHLers, past and present, along with other domestic stars, are regularly spotted at **BARFLY (Mikonkatu 15/+358.9.687.7360)**, which is next door to rock bar **ON THE ROCKS (+358.9.6122.030)**. **TEATTERI KLUBI (Pohjoisesplanadi 2/ +358.9.681.1130)** (see listing under **A Bit of Soho**), the second-floor nightclub of Teatteri restaurant, hosts a mix of regular folk and celebrities.

Grooving Cool DJs play **BAR CAFÉ ALAHUONE (Mannerheimintie 13A/+358.9.440.017)** in the VR Makasiinit complex and **MOCAMBO (Ratakatu 9/+358.9.622.4960)** hosts bundolo.net (www.bundolo.info), a dance club on Friday and Saturday nights from 10 pm to 4 am featuring funk, soul, and reggae. **HIGHLIGHT CAFE (Fredrikinkatu 42/+358.9.7345.822)**, in a spacious well-restored old church, is a multi-level mainstream venue. Further down the street is **VANHA MAESTRO (Fredrikinkatu 51-53/+358.9.612.9900)**, the place to go for traditional Finnish dancing, including the *humppa,* a Finnish couples dance distantly related to waltz and tango. The old Maestro tends to draw an older crowd, but people of all ages are always to be found there. The club's daytime dances are popular with seniors.

Music

Rock and Pop Finland has long had a healthy rock music industry, but until recently, with a few exceptions such as glam rockers Hanoi Rocks, parody band Leningrad Cowboys, and quirky 22-Pistepirkko, the industry's success has been largely domestic. One of the main exporting challenges is linguistic — Finnish is not exactly a world language.

However, during the past decade growing numbers of Finnish bands have taken to singing in English, and have done so successfully with a fresh, global sound.

The arrival of MTV Nordic in 1998 provided Finnish rock with a new international launching pad. In 2000, Bomfunk MC's "Freestyler," an infectious mix of hip-hop and chemical beats, went to the top of the charts in ten countries. HIM, fronted by Ville Valo, a sexy, young goth Iggy Pop, sold a million copies of its second album *Razorblade Romance*. Darude's 1999 "Sandstorm," which initially swept the UK and Ibiza dance circuit, is still being played around the world.

Ones to watch as the next big Finn thing — Kemopetrol fronted by Laura Närhi; The Crash; LAB; The Flaming Sideburns, a cross between punk thrash and garage soul touted by rock music bible *Rolling Stone*; Sweatmaster, Spinal Tap meets the

Hives according to music mag *NME;* Children of Bodom; all-girl band Thee Ultra Bimboos; Giant Robot; Lemonator; The Rasmus; Kwan; and Lordi — the list goes on.

Lord of lounge Jimi Tenor, whose real name is decidedly less catchy (it's Lassi Lehto), a long-time Londoner who lives in Barcelona these days, is part of the international wave of successful Finnish electronic fusion musicians. Others include Pan Sonic, much-lauded NuSpirit Helsinki, a DJ collective with a jazzy sound, and DJ Jori Hulkkonen — you have to hand it to someone who made Corey Hart's '80s hit, "Sunglasses at Night," cool again.

Finnish Music in Finnish Local artists hold about 40 per cent of the domestic market, which is unusual for a small European country. If you want to sample truly Finnish rock, listen to domestic faves such as J. Karjalainen, who captures the essence of Finnishness with ballads about melancholia and broken hearts; Leevi and the Leavings; Hector; Juice Leskinen; Popeda; Eppu Normaali; Suurlähettiläät; or Ultra Bra. Ultra Bra's weave of witty, political lyrics still gets airplay, although the group is no longer together under that name. Some former Ultra Bra members are part of the Scandinavian Music Group, which sings in Finnish.

Rock Spots and Rock Stars

BAR LOOSE (Fredrikinkatu 34/+358.9.586.1819) is the best place to go for an unstaged rock 'n' roll experience and to rub shoulders with Finnish rocksters from members of all-girl band Thee Ultra Bimboos to Ville Valo (lead singer of HIM), and the Flaming Sideburns. Only music in English is played, and the barstaff are all bona fide band members.

Live music aficionados need go no further than **TAVAS-TIA** (Urho Kekkosenkatu 4-6/+358.9.694.8511/www.tavastiaklubi.fi), one of the oldest rock venues in the country with live

music just about every night of the week. Their typical line-up for a four-week stretch includes J. Karjalainen, 22-Pistepirkko, The Flaming Sideburns, HIM, Nu-Spirit Helsinki, and Hector. Tavastia's website is one of the few Finnish bar/club sites that is available almost entirely in English.

NOSTURI (Telakkakatu 8/+358.9.681.1880) is the new home of Elmu, the live music association, which was for years in Lepakko, a building that was demolished when the Ruoholahti area was redeveloped. Nosturi has a special alcohol-free zone where minors are allowed for concerts featuring bands with under-age appeal.

The Joy of Jazz   Although jazz has been a part of the Finnish music scene since the 1920s, the first generation of full-time jazz musicians didn't appear on the scene until the 1960s. But it's an area that's rapidly growing. Names to watch for include the UMO Jazz Orchestra, Pekka Pohjola, Rinne Radio, Krakatau, Trio Töykeät, Lenni-Kalle Taipale, hepcats the U-Street All Stars, and clarinetist and saxophonist Antti Sarpila, whose Antti Sarpila Swing Band has a unique, big band meets opera sound.

Jazz Joints   The home of live jazz, **STORYVILLE** (Museokatu 8/ +358.9.408.007/www.storyville.fi), just behind the Parliament Buildings, is one of the few jazz joints open late — till 4 am — Monday through Saturday. From the Wade Mik-

kola Quartet to jazz groups from abroad, there's a cosmopolitan selection of music on the slate. Storyville's piano
bar features excellent pianists just about every night of
the week. **JUMO JAZZ CLUB** (Pursimiehenkatu 6/+358.9.6122.1914/
www.umo.fi) is home to the UMO jazz orchestra and
showcases live jazz from mainstream to avant-garde,
Latin, pop, and world music. Both the Storyville and
Jumo websites have some listings info in English. Other
venues around town that host regular jazz evenings include Kappeli's **CELLAR BAR** (Kellari Baari) (Eteläesplanadi
1/+358.9.681.244) and restaurant **JUTTUTUPA** (Säästöpankinranta
6/+358.9.774.48.60), with its Rytmihäiriö jazz club.

World Music   Vocal group Värttinä, which recently celebrated its 20th anniversary, has been a major international
success story with its world music chart-topping hits.
Techno accordionist Kimmo Pohjonen has been pegged
as the next big thing by the *Sunday Times* for the revolu-
tionary way that he plays the accordion.

Classical and Opera   Finland's prodigious classical output is
not in proportion to its relatively small population. Composer Jean Sibelius (1865–1957) was a musical genius and
champion of a nation fighting for independence, whose
best-known works include *Finlandia, Kullervo, Karelia,*
and *Tapiola.* Other significant 20th-century composers
include Joonas Kokkonen, Aulis Sallinen, and Einojuhani
Rautavaara.

   Top Finnish conductors on the international circuit

today include Esa-Pekka Salonen, Jukka-Pekka Saraste, Osmo Vänskä, and Mikko Franck; important composers include Magnus Lindberg and Kaija Saariaho. The international opera world is also rich with Finns including Matti Salminen, Jorma Hynninen, Monica Groop, and Karita Mattila. And who can forget the resonant voice of the late Martti Talvela?

Classical Venues

Scandinavia's oldest symphony orchestra, the Helsinki Philharmonic (www.hel.fi/filharmonia), under the direction of Leif Segerstam, holds its concerts at FINLANDIA HALL (Mannerheimintie 13E/+358.9.40.241/www.finlandia.hel.fi). The SIBELIUS ACADEMY (Pohjoinen Rautatie 9/+358.9.405.441) and KULTTUURITALO (Sturenkatu 4/+358.9.774.0270) are also venues for classical music. TEMPPELIAUKIO CHURCH (Lutherinkatu 3/+358.9.494.698) has organ music concerts, as do many of the churches around town, particularly on national holidays and Sundays.

As there are too many orchestras and groups to mention, classical music fans are best served by visiting www.musicfinland.com/classical, an excellent English-language site that gives background information, concert schedules, and ticket purchasing links.

The free listings guide, *Helsinki This Week,* which is available in hotels, cafés and shops around town, also lists concerts (and other events) in English. Tickets for concerts at larger venues are available through LIPPUPALVELU (TICKET SERVICE FINLAND), which has an English-language web service at www.ticketservicefinland.fi, or LIPPUPISTE at www.lippupiste.com(+358.600.900.900).

5.

Shopping

The Basics Helsinki can be a shopper's paradise if you know where to go. What isn't available in luxury brands — there's no Vuitton or Prada boutique — is more than made up for with the large selection of exotic Finnish labels, design wares, and the wide selection of international brands from InWear to Armani.

All stores list prices in euros — 1 euro is roughly equivalent to 1 US dollar — and a few shops still list prices in Finnish marks (FIM or mk) as well, even though it is no longer a valid currency. Because of the relative newness of the euro, many Finns still refer to prices in old money (1 euro is almost 6 Finnish marks).

The price on the tag includes 22 per cent value added tax (VAT), but if you are from a non-EU country, various tax rebate schemes are offered whereby you can get a tax refund if your purchases total 42 euros or more.

Most stores are open from 9 or 10 am to 6, 8, or 9 pm

weekdays, and until 5 or 6 pm on Saturdays, though some shops close as early as 2 or 3 pm on Saturdays. The 24-hour clock is used here, thus 6 pm is 18:00, 8 pm is 20:00, and so on. With the exception of the downtown core, stores tend to be closed on Sundays. In the summertime and around Christmas, larger stores may be open from 12 to 6 pm on Sundays. If you're in a pinch for food, pharmacy, or other items, the shops below the Railway Station are open every day including Sunday until 10 pm.

Big end-of-season sales take place in January/February and July/August, just after two of the most important holidays on the Finnish calendar: Christmas *(joulu)*, and midsummer *(juhannus)*. Smaller sales and special offers take place throughout the year.

Shopping is relatively pressure-free; the aggressive sales associates who work shop floors in other parts of the world don't, for the most part, seem to exist here.

For serious shoppers, the two most important words are the Finnish and Swedish words for "sale," which are *ale* and *rea,* respectively.

MORE DASH THAN CASH
Flea Markets
A great way to get a handle on the cultural anthropology of a place is through its flea markets and thrift shops, where a society's artefacts are on display.

Flea markets can be a diamonds-in-the-dust game. Sometimes there's just plain junk for sale, at other times you can make amazing scores and kit yourself out with a whole new wardrobe. Because we live in times where everything is disposable, second-hand can mean that something practically brand new is up for grabs for next to nothing.

At Helsinki flea markets, people may chat as they try to encourage you to buy, but they are rarely pushy, so you can browse without too much hassle. Naturally, haggling is part of the flea market game.

If you're looking for vintage design wears by Marimekko, Iittala glassware, or Arabia ceramics, flea markets are great places to look. However, sellers are usually aware of the value of these items, so while you won't get ripped off, you're unlikely to score such treasures for next to nothing.

In Finnish, *kirpputori* means "flea market" and is used to denote both markets and thrift or charity shops. One

89

of the oldest and best in town is the outdoor **HIETANIEMI FLEA MARKET** at the Hietaniemi Square just at the west end of Bulevardi. It's open year round during the day, Monday through Saturday. During the summer months, there's an evening market, Monday to Friday from 3:30 to 8 pm, and a Sunday day market. Here you can find books, watches, clothes, dishes, and other odds and ends.

Flea markets are great places to look for pre-loved Finnish design.

There are some professional sellers (who are regulars at several of the city's flea markets) whose wares look as though they've come directly from a shop floor. Their prices tend to be high, though reasonable compared with what you'd pay in a store.

The best deals are from vendors emptying their attics or doing spring-cleaning, who simply want to get rid of stuff. Although the selection is plentiful during the market's initial opening hours, the advantage of coming to the evening market just before closing, say after 7 pm, is that the prices drop dramatically. Most sellers would rather make a quick (cheap) sale than cart everything back home.

VALLILA (Aleksis Kivenkatu 17), or **VALTTERI** as it's known, is Finland's largest year-round indoor flea market, which is open seven days a week inside a hall that was once a railway cargo warehouse. Many of the merchants are regular folk selling the contents of their attics or closets — lots of clothing here — and their prices can be very reasonable.

THE VR FLEA MARKET (Mannerheimintie 13) at the VR Makasii-nit complex runs on Saturdays and Sundays from about 9 in the morning until 2 or 3 in the afternoon. Located just steps from the modern art museum, Kiasma, these build-ings were once stables where the Russian army troops kept their horses when Finland was under tsarist rule in the early 1900s. Although the market runs into the after-noon, it's best visited before noon as many sellers start taking down their stalls around lunch time. Here you can find glassware, ceramics, jewellery, clothing, books, and electronics.

Thrift Stores

Thrift stores such as those run by the Salvation Army *(Pelastusarmeija)* and other benevolent organisa-tions often have a set rate for items, regardless of whether they're designer or not.

In the Kallio neighbourhood, there are two thrift shops run by **FIDA LÄHETYSTORI**, one at **Kolmas linja 3 (+358.9.773.6635)** and the other a five-minute walk away, on the second floor of **Hämeentie 31 (+358.9.701.4772)**. From the Hämeentie shop, just down the street and around the corner is the **PELAS-TUSARMEIJAN KIRPPUTORI** (Pääskylänrinne 3/+358.9.762.684), tucked away on a quiet side street. It's one of the few thrift stores where you might find a Marimekko shirt for 3 euros or other Finnish brands like Nanso and Finnwear, as well as dishes, furniture, and children's clothing.

Kaurismäki film fans will recognise this Salvation Army store as one of the key locations in 2002's award-winning *Man Without a Past,* the story of a man who suffers a blow to the head and amnesia, and then falls in love with Kati Outinen, who plays a Salvation Army worker.

Downtown, there's another popular **FIDA LÄHETYSTORI SHOP (Iso Roobertinkatu 24/+358.9.612.1770)** that sells previously owned furniture, books, and clothing. It often has a good selection of stuff, likely owing to its location in trendy Punavuori, which happens to be the neighbourhood where *Kotikatu* ("Home Street"), the Finnish *Coronation Street,* is filmed.

Consignment and Vintage

One of the city's best consignment stores — big selection and reasonable prices — is **RUUTU ROUVA (Fredrikinkatu 16/+358.9.174.726)**, run by Raili Leino, who is one of the city's friendliest shop keepers. Her store brims (literally, it's so packed you can hardly move) with designer and vintage finds from Prada and Ferragamo to Finnish brands such as Rils, Rintala, and Ritva Falla. A favourite among models and fashionistas of all ages, Ruutu Rouva also sells Finnish national costumes.

Not far away, **KAUNIS VEERA (Albertinkatu 10/+358.9.622.4091)** stocks a good selection of pre-loved women's brand labels — Finnish and international.

PENNY LANE (Runeberginkatu 37/+358.9.499.412) in Töölö features a choice of vintage and more current lines such as

Diesel and DKNY, and is frequented by a youngish crowd. **PLAY IT AGAIN SAM** (Rauhankatu 2/+358.9.628.877) in Kruununhaka carries evening wear and jewellery; the city's set designers, photographers, and artists come to Sam's to create authentic period pieces for both men and women.

DEPARTMENT STORES AND MALLS
Shop Till You Drop

STOCKMANN (Aleksanterinkatu 52/+358.9.1211), Northern Europe's largest department store, is right up there with the world's leading department stores including London's Harrods, Paris's Galleries Lafayettes, and New York's Saks Fifth Avenue.

Stokka, as it's known, has been around since the 1860s, and is a city centrepoint. One of Helsinki's most popular meeting spots is under the Stockmann's clock on Aleksanterinkatu.

Inside, seven glorious floors circle the two open foyers that run from the ground floor up and sell everything from perfume, jewellery, and watches to clothing, housewares, electronics, and food. In-store restaurants and cafés provide necessary refuelling. You can easily spend a whole day here; some people do.

Stockmann still has a bit of a reputation as a place where better folk shop, a carry-over from the days when wealthy, aristocratic Swedish-speaking Finns were its main clientele. Though the store stocks high-end domestic and international brands, a lot of mid-range and downright affordable stuff is available, too.

The multilingual staff (22 languages are spoken, including Chinese and Arabic) wear small flags on their name-tags indicating which languages they speak. Devotion to customer service is legendary, and

Custom-made shoes, perfect fit.

the PA announcements — "Would the customer looking for a leopard print mobile phone cover please return to the electronics department?" — are often entertaining, in part because they're broadcast in several languages.

Stockmann has an entire floor devoted to women's clothing and carries fabulous Finnish labels such as Rils and recently revitalised Nanso, and quality Euro brands such as Sand, Filippa K, Burberry, Marella, and Escada.

Menswear, on the second floor, is equally diverse, with labels such as Hugo Boss, Filippa K for Men, Burb-

erry, and Matinique. The home and giftware section with glassware by Iittala, dishes by Arabia, and porcelain by Rörstrand, is often packed with tourists. The store has a great export service that will parcel and post your tax-free purchases so that you don't need to lug them home.

Bargain-hunters pop into the fifth-floor Löytöpiste (literally "find spot"), where clothing and accessories from previous seasons are sold at a discount.

Latino popstar Ricky Martin was on hand to sign autographs when Stockmann's hip basement — with CD and electronics, trendy Kitchen restaurant, and One

Way clothing shop — opened a few years ago. Technically across the street, One Way connects to Stockmann's via an underground tunnel. Aimed at the tweenie and early twenties set, One Way stocks Diesel, Pepe, Camper, Carhartt, and [ES TI: CI:] and STC, its own affordable line of jeans, sweaters, jackets, and T-shirts, styled after pricier labels.

Another underground passage — albeit long and winding — links Stockmann to the **Forum Shopping Complex (Mannerheimintie 20)**, which was Finland's first shopping mall when it opened in the early '80s. With 120 shops on several levels, you can find clothing, sportswear, leather goods, electronics, and giftware here. Shops include Iittala, Sisley, Vero Moda, The Body Shop, and Seppälä. The basement-level food court has a decent selection of fast food.

Upmarket **Kämp Galleria (Pohjoisesplanadi 37)** houses Helsinki's huge flagship Marimekko and H&M stores, and close to 50 boutiques including Lacoste, Diesel, Bam-Bami (where the city's best-dressed kids are outfitted), and Zio, which carries the deliciously whimsical Muxart line of shoes from Barcelona.

Further down the street, the **Kluuvi** shopping complex **(Aleksanterinkatu 9)** once housed Max Mara and other upscale brands, but these days it's home to a mix of mid-range shops such as Indiska, an Eastern-themed home décor and clothing emporium, Halonen (a Finnish C&A), and some fast food restaurants.

The functionalist style **Sokos** department store building **(Mannerheimintie 9/ +358.10.765.000)** was finished just in time for the 1952 Olympics. Sokos carries clothing and footwear for men, women, and children, along with housewares, and smaller items such as cosmetics. Its large, basement foodstore, S-Market, is open until 10 pm every night. **ALEKSI 13** (Aleksanterinkatu 13/+358.9.131.441) is smaller than Sokos, focussing on clothing, shoes, and accessories for the whole family. Here you'll find international and Finnish labels, including a good selection of quality sporty wear by Luhta.

Scandinavia's largest shopping mall, **ITÄKESKUS** (+358.9.343.1005), is about a ten-minute metro ride from downtown. (Take the metro to the Itäkeskus station.) There are 240 stores including a mini Stockmann, and about 30 eateries.

CLOTHING
Scandinavia's Gap

H&M (Aleksanterinkatu 42 A/+358.9.684.4170), in the Kämp Galleria and several other locations including Forum and Itäkeskus, is Hennes & Mauritz, the Swedish mega chain that has been giving the Gap a run for its money in other parts of the world. (There are no Gap stores in Scandinavia.) H&M is great for stocking up on basics such as T-shirts, trousers, and tops for men and women at prices that won't break the bank. There are loads of accessories from sparkly barrettes to purses, as well as trendy pieces that imitate the latest catwalk fashions. Across the street, **H&M JUNIOR** (Aleksanterinkatu 11/+358.9.687.7690) sells great stuff for kids.

Another Swedish company, **LINDEX (Aleksanterinkatu 15/ +358.9.0201.422.453)**, with several other locations including those in Forum and Itäkeskus, sells an assortment of affordable basics, from T-shirts, underwear, and sweaters, to slacks and skirts for women and children. An added bonus — they carry plus sizes.

Boutiques If you are looking for good quality clothing and accessories in the mid-price range, Helsinki is a great place to shop for unique one-off pieces whether your style is classic or avant-garde.

Fresh Young Things   IvanaHelsinki founder and designer Paola Suhonen is one of the hottest names in Finnish fashion, both at home and abroad. Sold in eleven countries, the playful IvanaHelsinki label takes a '70s camping theme and gives practical pieces a retro, Scandi design twist. **IVANAHELSINKI CAMPUS** (Uudenmaankatu 15/+358.9.622.4422) is worth visiting for the store's funky mural alone.

Suhonen, also a freelance designer who recently helped revamp Finnish label Nanso, is one of the founders of **LIIKE** (Yrjönkatu 25/+358.9.646.265), another boutique with a smart, young sensibility. *Liike* means "business," "store," and "movement" in Finnish, so the shop's name conveys a tongue-in-cheek quality; it's like calling your store, well, store. The small shop showcases modern lines and one-off pieces by designers Merja Seitsonen, Johanna Vainio, Anu Leinonen, IvanaHelsinki, and Lustwear.

LIMBO (Annankatu 13/+358.9.644.060) sells its own hip Limbo label, whimsical casual wear for guys and gals designed by two young women.

A skate shop for girls, **STONE 15** (Uudenmaankatu 15/+358.9.6922.135) shares the same address as IvanaHelsinki and carries Airwalk, Swedish label Svea, and Icelandic label Nikita. (**PONKE'S THE SHOP** in the Kluuvi shopping complex sells skatewear for guys.) Check out **BEAMHILL** (Yliopistonkatu 7/+358.9.622.2653) for streetwear by Replay, Acne, Nudie, and smaller labels such as Encore, and Twin, a Porvoo-based line that makes groovy little handbags. Yliopistonkatu (University Street) runs into Ateneuminkuja (Ateneum's Lane), which also has several clothing boutiques with a youngish sensibility including Serpentiini and Sisters.

99

Freda In addition to oodles of great clothing shops along Fredrikinkatu, known as "Freda" to the locals, there are also several good shoe stores along the street.

IVO NIKKOLO (Fredrinkinkatu 32/+358.9.685.3884) is a mid-size boutique featuring well tailored, classic clothing for work and play by the eponymous Estonian designer. Across the street, **GAUDETE (Fredrikinkatu 35/+358.9.608.635)** stocks Calvin Klein, Burberry, FCUK, and Filippa K for men and women, and Finnish designer Hanna Sarén's nifty creations, which are sold at New York's tony Takashimaya department store. Sarén's wooden sandals have appeared on *Sex and the City,* worn by the TV show's main character, Carrie Bradshaw, played by Sarah Jessica Parker.

The exotic mix of Finnish and European design labels for men and women at **ASUNA (Fredrikinkatu 24/+358.9.611.543)** is also worth checking out.

Style Council Italian **MAX MARA (Aleksanterinkatu 11/+358.9.177.377)** carries the refined elegance of the various Max Mara lines, while **DELLA MARGA (Pohjoisesplanadi 33/+358.9.2600.265)** has a good selection of big name French, American, and Italian labels including Sonia Rykiel, Armani, D&G, and Krizia. The Esplanade has several high-end clothing boutiques, and just off the south side,

Boutique Kaarina K (Kasarmikatu 25/+358.9.633.901), owned by Kaarina Kivilahti, well known in Finnish society circles, stocks luxury labels including Charles Jourdan, Moschino, Versace, Lacroix, and Karl Lagerfeld.

Spanish success story of the decade, **Zara** (Aleksanterinkatu 19/+358.9.253.00300) forever bustles as the city's young fashionistas jockey for copies of high-end lines at cut-rate prices.

High Street On Korkeavuorenkatu, a street that runs up into the tony Eira neighbourhood, there are several restaurants and cafés, antique shops, homeware stores, and choice clothing boutiques.

Stepping into **Valkoinen Elefantti** (Korkeavuorenkatu 3/+358.9.611.038) is like entering a clothing spa: It always smells nice and the subdued white décor is calming. The women's clothing is exquisite; dresses, tops, trousers, and skirts in silk, linen, lace, cotton, and wool can be paired with shoes and bags in materials ranging from suede to bejewelled fabric. Finnish brand Muotikuu is the shop's main line. **LILLY** (Korkeavuorenkatu 11/+358.9.635.992) carries Mulberry and other quality lines while across the street, Lilly 2 sells the previous season's stock — shoes and clothing — at a substantial discount.

Around the corner, **ILONA PELLI** (Tarkk'ampujankatu 1/ +358.9.625.664) showcases the award-winning clothes of designer Ilona Pelli, who is known for her high-quality minimalist creations.

Men's Club

Department stores Stockmann, Sokos, and Aleksi 13 carry a broad selection of clothing and shoes for men, as do Beamhill, One Way, and H&M.

LEFT FOOT COMPANY (Sanomatalo/+358.9.278.2916) is a male shoe-shopping dream. (If men have any fantasies about shopping.) The Finnish company custom makes their stylish shoes and once you've had your feet measured by laser and picked out tops and bottoms (type and colour of leather), the made-to-order footwear can be picked up or shipped directly to you. You can order further pairs online or by phone, without ever having to visit a shoe store again.

UNION 5 MALE (Erottajankatu 15–17/+358.9.648.818) stocks well-known brands, local and international, and is geared towards guys who have outgrown the skateboarder look, but aren't ready to move to a more formal look. At **UNION 5** next door, there's plenty of casual wear for a youngish urban crowd, male and female.

Well-made suits and accessories are best found at Brioni-central **FERE** (Bulevardi 3/+358.9.6121.578), classic **HUGO BOSS** (Eteläesplanadi 24/+358.9.612.42.910), or at **SOLO** (Fredrikinkatu 24/+358.9.611.616), which also has a store in **ATENEUMINKUJA** (+358.9.6969.3069). Stylish **SEVEN** (Eerikinkatu 5/+358.9.6944253) carries Calvin Klein and Hugo Boss for men and women.

Further down the same street as Seven, **KONEHELSINKI** (Eerikinkatu 46/+358.694.5505) sells the KoneHelsinki label, which is designed and made by the store's two male founders in their adjacent workshop. The store carries edgy asymmetrical T-shirts, jeans, tops, and toques as well as jewellery fashioned out of leather for men and women. New threads are brought out on the first Monday of each month.

Shoes and Bags

Deliciously named **KENKÄ FRIIKKI** (Eerikinkatu 1/+358.9.683.193.80), which means "shoe freak" in Finnish, has a wide selection of well-made classic and trendy Italian women's shoes, mules, boots, and heels. **RIZZO** (Aleksanterinkatu 46/+358.9.6229.2420) sells the Rizzo line of shoes for men and women, and stocks well-known European brands such as Sergio Rossi and Free Lance. **LA MATTA** (Unioninkatu 21/+358.9.626.005), just off the Esplanade in a slickly designed bright space, sells high-end Italian women's shoes by Farrutx, Casadei, and Armando Pollini in the 100 to 300 euro range. Campus fave Superga is also available, as are bags and wallets by Coccinelle.

Favoured by those over 40, Finnish footwear and bags designed by Pertti Palmroth are available at **PERTTI PALMROTH** boutiques in many locations around town, including Pohjoisesplanadi 37 (+358.9.628.252).

RED SHOE (Fredrikinkatu 45/+358.9.604.670), so-named for its founder Paula Lassila's favourite colour, sells shoes and bags made in Italy for the Red Shoe label, in a range of different colours with many options in the perennial favourite, black.

Bag heaven **LONGCHAMP** (Pohjoisesplanadi 27/+358.9.622.1252) seems to bring out new styles almost weekly. Longchamp, which is for Europeans what Coach and Kate Spade bags are for Americans, is also sold at M-Boxi in the Kämp Galleria. Longchamp fold-up travel bags are ubiquitous in airports throughout Europe, and the chic leather and fabric purses, bags, and luggage, are all made in France.

info

FINNISH DESIGN   Renowned the world over, Finnish design made its official international debut in the '50s. At the 1951 Milan Triennale, Finland won a quarter of the medals on offer and designers Kaj Frank, Tapio Wirkkala, and Timo Sarpaneva became known abroad.

Finnish design is synonymous with several names including visionary architect and interior designer Alvar Aalto (1898–1976). His organic functionalist style is the perfect example of Finnish design: Form follows practical function with nature both as an inspiration and a material.

Marimekko, founded in 1951 by Armi Ratia and launched at Helsinki's then-most fashionable restaurant Kalastajatorppa, was a lifestyle concept before such a concept existed. Folksy cotton brights in fabrics, clothing, and homewares for the whole family lit up Finland after the devastation and bleakness of the Second World War.

Jackie Kennedy fell in ♥ with Marimekko.

Ratia marketed Marimek-ko to the world, and it was a fabulous stroke of good fortune that former first lady Jackie Kennedy fell in love with Marimekko, which launched in the US in the '60s. Kennedy had been criticised for wearing expensive Parisian fashions; when she donned a sensible Marimekko dress on the cover of *Sports Illustrated,* the syndicated story ran in 300 American newspapers.

Function and durability are paramount in Finnish design. Forever-in-style glassware by Iittala and ceramics by Arabia appear in interior and design magazines spreads around the world.

If there is a common thread that runs through Finnish design, it's heeding environmental values, using natural materials, and ensuring that the manufacturing process is as unharmful to the environment as possible. Products are well made and stand the test of time.

For design devotees, *Form Function Finland,* a quarterly magazine in English, provides a good overview of Finnish design.

Design Boutiques

DESIGNOR (Pohjoisesplanadi 25/+358. 9.0204.39.11) sells tableware, glass, and cutlery, with classic lines by Iittala (glassware), Arabia (porcelain), Hackman (stainless steel pots, pans, and flatware), and Rörstrand, whose Stripey Origo line has been a huge hit.

Along the Esplanade, there are three MARIMEKKO SHOPS including the flagship store at Pohjoisesplanadi 31 (+358.9.686.0240), which is part of the Kämp Galleria. Many a foreigner has wondered who Marimekko is — the word simply means "Mary's dress" in Finnish. Marimekko's trademark multicoloured prints and folksy florals are perpetually in, as are their durable clothes, bags, towels, fabrics, and sheets. At the Marimekko shop next door to the Swedish Theatre, there's often a discount bin tucked around the corner with cosmetics bags, slippers, T-shirts, and other items on sale for up to half the original price.

Also along Pohjoisesplanadi, at 23, 25, and 27, respectively, Finnish designer clothing labels ANNIKKI KARVINEN, RILS, and VUOKKO have boutiques. Just off the Esplanade, the snazzy **NANSO** store (Mikonkatu 2/+358.201258261), designed by Kaisa Blomstedt, carries the Nanso line of retro-inspired casual wear and accessories.

Thoroughly modern **ARTEK** (Eteläesplanadi 18/+358.9.613.250) opened in 1935 to sell furniture by Alvar Aalto. In addition to original Aalto designs — his Easy Chair 400 is perennial stock — furniture by other Finnish designers is also available, along with tableware, carpets, and fabrics. Artek carries Snowcrash, and Tonfisk, a modern line of practical items such as storage jars, salt and pepper shakers, and espresso cups, all made using wind power to generate the electricity for firing up kilns.

FORMWERK (Annankatu 5/+358.9.6214.611) sells smart interior homeware, as does **SKANNO** (Kluuvikatu 2/+358.9.612.9440), which also showcases the latest in furniture design and

smaller gifty items. Anu Pentik's eponymous **PENTIK (Mannerheimintie 5/+358.9.6124.0795 and other locations)** is like an upscale Scandi Martha Stewart Home, with beautiful ceramic dishes, textiles, and lovely teddy bears.

Jewellery and Handicrafts

SUOMEN KÄSITYÖN YSTÄVÄT (Runeberginkatu 40/+358.9.612.6050), the Friends of Finnish Handicraft, showcases handicrafts made by Finnish artists. This is a great place to get affordable one-off or limited edition gifts. Sauna accessories — from pine soap to wooden pails — and a wide variety of hand-woven textiles and *ryijy*s, a traditional Finnish handmade wall tapestry, are available, along with *ryijy*-making kits starting at 10 euros.

TAITO SHOP HELSKY (Unioninkatu 21/+358.9.677.703) also sells handmade crafts for gifts or souvenirs. **RYIJYPALVELU (Abrahaminkatu 7/+358.9.660.615)** specialises in *ryijy* rugs and stocks *ryijy*-making supplies. **SAUNA SHOP (Eteläranta 14/+358.9.668.9970)** carries everything for the sauna.

Practical household utensils such as birch butter knives complement the range of wooden and silver jewellery and toys at **AARIKKA (Pohjoisesplanadi 27/+358.9.652.277)**, which got its start in 1954 when founder Kaija Aarikka designed five teak buttons for a dress. The buttons were a bigger hit than the dress; these days Aarikka is sold around the world.

KALEVALA KORU (Unioninkatu 30/+358.9.171.520) is better known for its jewellery, but it also carries handicrafts including knitwear in traditional and modern designs. Produced by top Finnish designers, its jewellery in bronze, silver, and gold is based on archaeological finds that date back to the 10th and 11th centuries. Kalevala Koru is sold in shops around town, and the company also makes Kaunis Koru, a modern line of rings, necklaces, and bracelets. **GALERIE BJÖRN WECKSTRÖM** (Kluuvikatu 2/+358.9.656.529) sells the nature-inspired Lapponia line, and **UNION DESIGN** (Eteläranta 14/+358.9.6220.0333) is a collective workshop of goldsmiths, silversmiths, and jewellers. Paula Nummela's **DPN** (Ateneuminkuja/+358.9.622.3722) sells the designer's modern and swelegant silver rings, necklaces, bracelets, and earrings.

Toys Kids love **FANNY AND ALEXANDER** in the **KISELEFF BAZAAR**, at the corner of Aleksanterinkatu 28 and Unioninkatu 27. From stickers to stuffed animals, toy cars, and miniature dollhouse furniture, this is European kidstuff at its best.

Kiseleff is home to more than 20 shops, which sell handicrafts such as jewellery, clothing, candles, and Christmas decorations. The cheery space was a sugar factory in the early 19th century, and from 1880 to 1930, it housed the Stockmann department store.

Stockmann has a large toy department on the sixth floor, and **TIIMARI**, with several locations around town including Kaivopiha, is an all-ages kidstore with cards, beaded bracelets, and sweet, kitschy little things. Kämp Galleria's **MOOMIN SHOP** (+358.9.622.2206) is full of Moomin goodies, from mugs to fridge magnets, and all of it, though totally commercial and touristy, manages to maintain a sense of the original spirit of author Tove Jansson's wonderful Moomintroll world.

CDs and Vinyl For one-stop music shopping, try Viiskulma (Five Corners), the intersection of five streets and the home of several music shops, which conjure up a *High Fidelity* feeling. **DIGELIUS** (Laivurinrinne 2/+358.9.666.375) carries an excellent selection of jazz, folk, traditional, and world music, and is known for its wonderfully knowledgeable and helpful service. Across the street, **POPPARIENKELI** (Fredrikinkatu 12/+358.9.661.638) sells pop, rock, and funk CDs, including hard-to-find Finnish albums, and British and American albums from the '60s and '70s. Nearby, **LIFESAVER** (Laivurinkatu 41/+358.9.630.051) stocks soul, house, funk, hip hop, disco, electronica, jazz, and some pre-loved vinyl.

A few streets over, funky and fabulous **STUPIDO SHOP** (Iso Roobertinkatu 20-22/+358.9.646.990) sells rock, hip hop, electronic, punk, indie, and vinyl, while **FENNICA RECORDS** (Albertinkatu 35/+358.9.685.1433) specialises in country, blues, and roots music, from the '50s to the '00s. Near Kaisaniemi metro station, **FUGA** (Kaisaniemenkatu 7/+358.9.7001.8251) features both classic and contemporary music.

FREE RECORD SHOP (Mannerheimintie 4/+358.9.6841680) is the largest record/CD shop in the city. **TUNNELIN LEVY** (+358.9.635.363), under the Railway Station, and **ANTTILA DEPARTMENT STORE** (the Finnish Wal-Mart), in the same complex, carry CDs. **STREET BEAT RECORDS** (Mikonkatu 8/+358.9.632.630) bills itself as the home of "music for the clubbing generation."

info   **FIN LIT 101**   Finns read — a lot. Per capita, Finland publishes more books than any other country. That's no small feat given that the potential market for Finnish books, most of which are in Finnish, is about 5 million readers. Library stats are equally impressive: Per capita, Finland has the highest number of registered book borrowers (more than half of its population) in the world.

Highlights of Finnish literature include the *Kalevala* (1835), a collection of poems which form the national epic and were compiled by Elias Lönnröt (1802–1884). Likened to Homer's *Iliad,* the *Kalevala* has several themes; its most important battles are waged with words rather than swords. It's about human relations – love, sex, wooing, and marriage. The women are strong and the men are often pathetic and weak.

Aleksis Kivi's 1870 *Seven Brothers (Seitsemän veljestä)* is regarded as one of the first Finnish novels of importance, while the international literary hit of all time is *Sinuhe the Egyptian (Sinuhe egyptiläinen)* by Mika Waltari (1908–1979), which has been translated into more than 30 languages, sold millions of copies, and landed on several bestseller lists.

F.E. Sillanpää won the Nobel prize for literature in 1939 for *Silja the Maid,* his portrayal of peasant life and nature. Prolific poet, journalist, and novelist Eino Leino is a national treasure whose literary legacy is evident around Helsinki. One of the country's best-loved poets is J.L. Runeberg, who penned the lyrics to the national anthem "Maamme," and is commemorated with a day of cake eating. Väino Linna's *The Unknown Soldier,* a critique of Finland's role in the Second World War, was initially dismissed by critics and went on to become a perennial domestic bestseller.

Children and adults alike treasure the Moomintroll series by Tove Jansson (1914–2001); her books and drawings have made their way around the world and are particularly popular in Japan.

Poet, playwright, and publisher Paavo Haavikko's work has appeared in French, German, and English, while poet Pentti Saarikoski (1937–1983), a talented *enfant terrible* who died of drink, was fluent in classical Greek and translated the work of Homer.

More recently, the younger generation of writers whose work has made it into the English-speaking world to favourable reviews include Monika Fagerholm, whose *Beautiful Women by the Sea* is an unsettling account of two young Finnish women's Americanised lives in the 1960s, and painter Rosa Liksom, who writes in a soft-core Kathy Acker vein.

Kjell Westö, whose award-winning *Kites Over Helsinki* chronicles the yuppie euphoria of the late '80s and the subsequent crash of the early '90s, has written several books (as of yet little of his work has been translated into English), which eloquently capture the struggles of contemporary Swedish-Finnish life.

English-language quarterly *Books from Finland* gives an informative overview of the literary scene and runs excerpts from forthcoming titles.

Books and Magazines Finland's largest bookshop, the **ACADEMIC BOOKSTORE (Pohjoisesplanadi 39/+358.9.121.41)**, stocks fiction, non-fiction, poetry, geography, travel, history, kidlit, and more. It's all here — and in more than 30 languages. If you're looking for Finnish literature in translation, this is a good place to start your search.

Downstairs, the basement-level stationary section carries a sizeable selection of office supplies, including Ord Nin G&R, a pricey but stylish line of notebooks, pens, pencils, cases, and bags from Sweden.

The street-level magazine and newspaper area shelves some 3000 titles from around the world, from fashion mags such as *Vogue* and *Elle* in numerous different language editions to news magazines and papers including *Time, The Economist, The Guardian, Herald Tribune,* and

Finns read — a lot.

FT. Specialist trade magazines such as *World Soccer* and *Flyer* are also sold here. On the main floor of Stockmann's department store (Mannerheimintie side), there's an equally well-stocked magazine and newspaper section.

Suomalainen Kirjakauppa (Aleksanterinkatu 23/+358.9.696. 2240), which translates to "the Finnish bookstore," also has a good selection of books, including novels and travel guides predominantly in Finnish and Swedish, but with choices in other languages, including English. **R-Kiosk** (Mannerheimintie 21-23/+358.9.496.064) has locations around town that are open till 9 or 10 pm. While the selection of magazines is mainly in Finnish and Swedish, there are titles in other languages. The **Railway Station R-Kiosk** is open until 10:30 pm seven nights a week and stocks about two dozen different foreign newspapers, including *Le Monde, La Repubblica*, and the *Independent*.

Antiquarian Bookshops

Though in fact not so very old, *Across Asia from East to West 1906–08* by explorer and former president Mannerheim is one of the most sought after titles in antiquarian bookshops. Published in 1940, a mere 500 copies were printed. Of those, only 100 were signed by the author. Foreigners and Finns search for the English-language edition because it contains scientific research about Asia that's not included in other language versions of the book.

Tourists and locals come to **Hagelstam** (Fredrikinkatu 35/ +358.9.649.291) to look for this and other titles. Hagelstam's valuable books collection comprises contemporary art books (Finnish design titles are especially popular), maps dating back to the 1600s, and Fennica from 1500 to 1800. Contemporary fiction and non-fiction in a variety of lan-

guages (including English) is also on the shelves.

Cecil Hagelstam runs the shop; his family's book-selling roots go back to the late 1890s.

Along Fredrikinkatu there are several antiquarian book-shops including **SYVÄ UNI** (Fredrikinkatu 55/+358.9.693.3939) and **KAMPINTORIN ANTIKVARIAATTI** (Fredrikinkatu 63/+358.9.694.3306). Kruununhaka's **LATERNA MAGICA** (Rauhankatu 7/+358.9.135.7559) is an art gallery and antiquarian store.

Possibly the city's most novel antiquarian outlet is a kiosk. Publisher and proprietor Timo Sinnemaa was inspired by the book kiosks along the banks of the River Seine in Paris and decided that Helsinki needed some-thing similar. Right next to Töölö's Elite restaurant, **KIRJALLINEN KIOSKI** (Runeberginkatu 45/+358.9.454.99.55) is open sporadically — largely depending on the weather — and sells non-fiction, poetry, and prose in Finnish, Swedish, and English (and the occasional title in French and Russian) for 3 to 5 euros.

Antiques

Several areas of town have a concentration of antique shops. **TOMORROW'S ANTIQUE** (Hietalahdenranta 11/+358.50.64.320) specialises in design furniture and lighting from 1930 to 1970. Here you'll find vintage Alvar Aalto, Tapio Wirkkala, Eero Saarinen, Timo Sarpaneva, and Eero Aarnio.

Some blocks away on Annankatu, which is rich in second-hand, vintage, antique, and retro finds, there's a cluster of stores including **ANTIK LINDBERG** (Annankatu 16/+358.9.647.901), specialising in furniture from the 18th and 19th centuries, **GALLERIE 1900** (Annankatu 11/+358.9.649.152), **OLD TIMES** (Annankatu 12/+358.9.604.606), and art shop **OSIRIS** (Annankatu 15/+358.9.603.420).

The well-heeled Kruununhaka neighbourhood has many antique-shop laden streets including Mariankatu, which starts just off the Esplanade, by the President's Palace, and continues up the hill. Noted by the *Louis Vuitton City Guide* series, **CLASSIC** (Mariankatu 13b/+358.9.625.171) deals in antiques and design. Further up the same street are **ALBERTIINA** (Mariankatu 24/+358.9.135.2855) and **ANTIIKKITUPA** (Mariankatu 26/+358.9.455.3936). Closer to Classic are **KARL FREDRIK** (Mariankatu 13b A/+358.9.630.014); **SALINPUOLI** (Mariankatu 14/+358.9.626.436); and **KAUNIS ARKI** (Mariankatu 17/+358.9.622.4521). Don't be discouraged by what must be the city's shortest opening hours — Tuesday through Thursday from 4 to 6 pm, and Saturday from 12 to 3 pm — Kaunis Arki's prices are very reasonable.

117

Foodstuffs The Market Square and Hakaniemi Square, and their respective indoor market halls, are great places to get fresh fruits and vegetables, fish, poultry, meat, bread, and baked goods. With the exception of the markets, you need to weigh your own fruits and veggies (sometimes sweets and pastries, too) — before you go to the grocery store checkout. The scale, which is almost always in the produce section, has a picture of each item. Push the right button and a sticker with the price pops out.

STOCKMANN'S DELI on the basement level of the department store (Aleksanterinkatu 52/+358.9.1211) is one of the best places in the city to grocery shop, not just for exotic delicacies (reindeer, camembert, caviar) but also for hard-to-find items that a foreigner might be sheepishly craving. Like peanut butter. Part of the fun of grocery shopping at Stockmann's deli is that it's schmooze central. Here the city's movers and shakers shop, from ambassadors and actors to Nokia's number one man, Jorma Ollila, and Kirsti Paakkanen, who heads Marimekko.

VIA (Ludviginkatu 8–10/+358.9.6811.3701) deli café prepares international food, from couscous salad to beet pasta, for eat in or takeaway, all made from fresh, healthy ingredients. Part of the same complex, Via restaurant, one of the city's trendiest eateries, is through the doors at the back of the deli.

For the budget-conscious, **ALEPA** (Asematunneli/ +358.9.657.032) has several locations around town including one under the Railway Station. Like the Price Choppers discount grocery chain, Alepa stocks food basics, but don't expect to find anything too exotic here. Some Alepa shops open as early as 7 am, and are open till 9 or 10 pm depending on the location and the day of the week. **S-Market** (Mannerheimintie 9/+358.9.622.0380) under the Sokos department store is open until 10 pm every night of the week.

Most grocery stores carry some organic (*luomu* in Finnish) products. For a good selection of organic food, try **Ruohonjuuri** (Mannerheimintie 13A/+358.9.445.465) in the VR Makasiinit complex, or the **S-Market** location at Kasarmikatu 19 (+358.9.622.6320).

Sample *salmiakki*, little, salted liquorice diamonds.

I Want Candy The orange and brown striped **Karkkipussi** (Aleksanterinkatu 50/+358.9.634.300 and others) shops around town offer a good assortment of sweets. For a particularly Finnish treat, sample the endless varieties of liquorice (*laku*), or try *salmiakki,* little, salted liquorice diamonds. R-Kiosks around town sell chocolate bars, gum, potato chips, and little grab bags of sweet and savoury goodies. **Stockmann** department store (Aleksanterinkatu 52/+358.9.1211) has a candy section on the ground floor with lots of Fazer confectionaries. **Fazer** (Kluuvikatu 3/+358.9.6159.2959) sells a mix of chocolates and sweets adjacent to its café, and grocery stores such as **Alepa, Valintatalo, S-Market,** and **Siwa** stock candy, as do gas stations and video rental shops. **Pick & Mix,** with locations in the Kaisaniemi and Rautatientori (+358.9.260.0488) metro stations, is a good place to get bulk bonbons for cheap.

119

Outlet Stores   The idea of outlet shopping is just starting to take off in Finland, but it's not quite on the same scale as it is in other parts of the world. While **STOCKMANN OUTLET** (Kuriiritie 17/+358.9.121.6551) isn't quite Filenes's Basement, it does sell the previous season's merchandise for 30 to 70 per cent off, with shoes, clothing, and accessories for men, women, and children. The outlet is a bit of a trek from downtown Helsinki; it's in the suburb of Vantaa, about a 20-minute train ride from the central Railway Station. (Get off at the Tikkurila Station and take bus 55 or 57, or take bus 611 or 611z from the Railway Station.)

Also in the Vantaa suburb, but not so near Stockmann Outlet, **DESIGNOR FACTORY SHOP** (Antaksentie 4/+358.204.39.3552) sells factory seconds of Iittala, Arabia, and Hackman at a discount. Better yet, the **ARABIA CENTRE** (Hämeentie 135/+358.204.39.3507) factory outlet, which is much closer to downtown Helsinki, unloads discontinued lines and slightly imperfect seconds of Arabia, Iittala, Hackman, and Rörstrand at a significant reduction. In the same complex, you'll find the Pentik outlet store and the Opa steelware outlet. Take the number 6 tram marked Arabia to the end of the line.

WAREHOUSE BRAND OUTLET (Itämerenkatu 21/+358.9.755.7300), in the Ruoholahti shopping centre (Ruoholahdenkauppakeskus) by the Ruoholahti metro station, stocks jeans, T-shirts, tops, coats, and skirts by labels including Gsusindustries and Guess, with runners and shoes by Converse, Clarks, and Swedish brand Vagabond, all at warehouse prices.

6.

Arts and Culture

Helsinki is an arts and culture positive capital, with many galleries and museums within walking distance of the city centre. Admission fees vary from free to 10 euros depending on the exhibition and venue. Children's admission is often free, or significantly reduced. Discounts are available with the Helsinki card (www.helsinkicard.com), which also offers price reductions on shows, sightseeing, and transportation and is available at the HELSINKI CITY TOURIST BUREAU (Pohjoisesplanadi 19/+358.9.169.3757), R-KI-OSKS, and other locations around town. Many museums and galleries are closed on Mondays, and open Tuesday through Sunday from 9 or 10 am to 6 or 8 pm; it's best to check specific opening hours as they vary.

GALLERIES AND MUSEUMS
Modern
KIASMA (Mannerheiminaukio 2/+358.9.1733.6501/ www.kiasma.fi), the Museum of Contemporary Art, exhibits

Finnish and international modern art from the 1960s to the present day. Designed by New York architect Steven Holl, Kiasma was the subject of much debate, partly because of its significant central location, its unusual shape, and because in a nation of designers, a foreigner's blueprints were chosen for the significant structure. But the award-winning success and overwhelming popularity of the 1998 building quashed most of the initial criticism.

The permanent collection includes work by Cindy Sherman and Andy Warhol, and leading Finnish artists such as homoerotic illustrator Touko Laaksonen, better known as Tom of Finland.

Kiasma's ultra-modern sleekness fits in with the glassy Sanomatalo, which is almost next door. In addition to stores, a café, and restaurants, Sanomatalo houses **DESIGN FORUM (+358.9.629.290/www.designforum.fi)**, a showroom and shop that displays all the latest in contemporary design. One floor down, **GALERIE ANHAVA (+358.9.669.989)** exhibits modern art of importance. Finland's largest newspaper, *Helsingin Sanomat,* the highest circulation daily in the Nordic region (450,000 copies sold daily), has its editorial offices in the same complex.

LASIPALATSI (Mannerheimintie 22–24/www.lasipalatsi.fi), the "glass palace," is a multi-media gallery from which the Finnish Broadcasting Corporation (YLE) broadcasts its breakfast television show. A fine example of 1930s functionalist style, the building is also home to experimental media, shops, cafés, and the BioRex movie cinema, one of the host venues for the annual Helsinki International Film Festival, Love and Anarchy. Lasipalatsi's city library branch won a Bill and Melinda Gates Foundation award a few years ago for its leading edge use of the Internet.

Just behind Lasipalatsi, about a two-minute walk away, is the **TENNIS PALACE** (Salomonkatu 15/+358.9.3108.7001/www.hel.fi/artmuseum) movie theatre and art complex, installed in what was once an indoor tennis hall. Part of the Helsinki City Museum, which has 11 museums around Helsinki, the Tennis Palace is known for exhibiting modern art and provocative international photography by photographers such as Araki and David Bailey.

Style-o-philes will appreciate **DESIGNMUSEO** (Korkeavuorenkatu 23/+358.9.622.0540/www.designmuseum.fi), the Finnish Museum of Art and Design, which has a permanent collection featuring design classics such as Eero Aarnio's famous Pastille chair, and over 35,000 objects, 40,000 drawings, and 100,000 images relating to the history of Finnish design. Exhibits run the gamut from homegrown talent to masters such as Frank Gehry and Pablo Picasso. Just around the corner is the **Museum of Finnish Architecture** (Kasarmikatu 24/+358.9.8567.5100/www.mfa.fi), with its impressive architectural archives and exhibition hall.

"Hey, this tram goes all the way to Arabia!" is a long-standing Helsinki joke. **Arabia Centre** (Hämeentie 135a/ +358.204.3911), the well-known ceramics factory, museum,

> # "Hey, this tram goes all the way to Arabia!"

and factory shop, is a 15 or 20-minute ride from the city centre. (Take tram number 6.) Utilising top Finnish designers, Arabia makes high-quality dishware. Its name came from the plot of land on which the factory was founded in the late 1800s — the original owner, a sea captain who travelled the world, named his plots of land after the places that he'd visited.

Next to Arabia is one the country's top art schools, the **University of Art and Design Helsinki** with its eighth-floor gallery, **Atski**, and student bar **Kipsari**, which is ever-popular with the art set.

This area, known as Arabianranta, or Arabia shore, aims to be the leading centre of art, design, and technology in the Baltic region by 2010. The goal of the Helsinki Virtual Village is to connect 12,000 residents, 9,000 jobs, and 6,000 students with one tool — the mobile phone, which will act as everything from a broadband browser to a smart wallet.

On the other side of town, **Kaapeli** (Tallberginkatu 1/

www.kaapelitehdas.fi) or the Cable Factory, was once a Nokia factory back when the company manufactured cable,
among other things. These days it's a massive arts complex with galleries, theatres, dance studios, a restaurant,
and café. More than 100 artists work in the Cable Factory's studios and workshops; Helsinki's Radio City and the
Finnish Museum of Photography are also headquartered
here.

Classics

ATENEUM (Kaivokatu 2/+358.9.1733.6401/www.ateneum.fi), the
Finnish National Gallery, is the majestic building opposite
the Railway Station Square. Designed by Theodore Hoi-
jer, the architect behind the swish Kämp Hotel, the 1887
building was recently extensively restored. You can catch
glimpses of the former colour scheme in the main stairwell
where a patch or two has been left to reveal the original
wall. Arguably one of the best art museums in Finland,
Ateneum showcases Finnish art from the 18th century to
the 1960s, with paintings by Helene Schjerfbeck, Hugo
Simberg, Pekka Halonen, Eero Järnefelt, and Akseli Gallen-Kallela, and foreign art from the 19th century to the
1960s by Cézanne, Gauguin, Van Gogh, Degas, and Rodin.

127

The other half of the National Gallery is in the equally
grand and recently renovated **SINEBRYCHOFF ART MUSEUM**
(Bulevardi 40/+358.9.173.361/www.fng.fi/), which comprises the
largest selection of Italian, Dutch, and Flemish paintings
in Finland, along with Russian and Karelian icons in silver,
china, and furniture from the 14th to mid-19th centuries.

Behind the Forum shopping complex, **AMOS ANDERSON ART MUSEUM** (Yrjönkatu 27/+358.9.6844.460/www.amosanderson.fi) boasts one of the city's largest private collections. Specialising in 20th century Finnish art, Anderson often exhibits work by young artists from other countries, as well as applied art, photography, and architecture. Amos Anderson, the museum's founder, was the owner of *Hufvudstadsbladet,* Finland's largest Swedish-language daily newspaper; the museum is housed in what was once his home.

The **NATIONAL MUSEUM OF FINLAND** (Mannerheimintie 34/ +358.9.405.01/www.nba.fi/natmus) looks more like a church than a museum. Designed in the National Romantic style by the architectural trio of Gesellius, Lindgren, and Saarinen, the museum presents archaeological, cultural, and ethnological acquisitions that chart the development of Finnish life from prehistoric times — people have lived in Finland since the Stone Age — to the present day.

Historic Homes

The **MANNERHEIM MUSEUM** (Kalliolinnantie 14/ +358.9.635.443/www.mannerheim-museo.fi) is the former home of marshal C.G.E. Mannerheim (1867–1951), president of Finland from 1944 to 1946, and one of the most influential characters in Finnish political history during the 20th century. At a time when Finland's political future was being carved out, Mannerheim supported close ties with Sweden and Western Europe and opposed Germany's national socialism.

The home, rented to the marshal by chocolate king Karl Fazer, is filled with Mannerheim memorabilia, including his medals, swords, uniforms, and antique furnishings. Soldier, politician, philanthropist, explorer, author, and all-around character — his 75th birthday party was crashed by Adolf Hitler — Mannerheim slept on an army cot by an open window, but sipped his morning café au lait from a Fabergé glass holder.

The museum chronicles the life of a statesman who fought in five wars, hunted tigers, and spoke eight languages from childhood (as an adult, he picked up an additional two: Polish and Chinese). Mannerheimintie, the city's main street, is named after him.

Steps away, the **CYGNAEUS ART GALLERY** (Kalliolinnantie 8/ +358.9.4050.9628/ www.nba.fi) is located in an elegant 1882 villa. One of Helsinki's few remaining wooden buildings, this was once the abode of Fredrik Cygnaeus, a professor who bequeathed his collection of predominantly Finnish 19th-century paintings and sculpture to the Finnish state. Many paintings by Ferdinand von Wright and some of Helene Schjerfbeck's work are on display.

Tamminiemi Villa, the official residence of president Urho Kekkonen during his presidency (1956–1981), houses the quirky **URHO KEKKONEN MUSEUM** (Seurasaarentie 15/+358.9.4050.9650). Kekkonen was Finland's longest serving president, and as a sign of respect from the Finnish people, he was allowed to stay on at Tamminiemi after he stepped down from the presidency. Here you'll find Finland's most famous sauna — it was the setting for some pivotal diplomatic meetings with Nikita Krushchev and other Soviet leaders during the Cold War.

On the outskirts of town, in the suburb of Espoo, the **GALLEN-KALLELA MUSEUM** (Tarvaspää, Gallen-Kallelantie 27, Espoo/ +358.9.541.3388/www.gallen-kallela.fi) is hidden in the woods.

Known as Tarvaspää, the home-studio-castle of Akseli Gallen-Kallela (1865–1931) was built between 1911 and 1913 by the artist. Gallen-Kallela is best known for his paintings from the *Kalevala*, the Finnish national epic. He also helped design the Finnish pavilion at the Paris Expo in 1900, and was very influential in the European arts scene.

On a pop culture note, scenes from *Billion Dollar Brain*, based on a novel by thriller writer Len Deighton, were filmed here in 1967, with British actor Michael Caine starring in the leading role and Tarvaspää acting as a luxurious lovenest.

Beside the museum, which features a large collection of Gallen-Kallela's paintings, graphics, and posters, there's a delightful café in an old 1850s villa that looks out over the inlet. The best way to get to the museum is to take tram number 4 to Munkkiniemi and then walk along the seaside for about three kilometres through the woods. There's also a bus (number 33) that runs to the museum from Munkkiniemi.

ALVAR AALTO'S FORMER HOME AND OFFICE in Helsinki's Munkkiniemi (Riihitie 20/+358.9. 480.123) recently opened to the public. The building was designed by Aino and Alvar Aalto, and much of its modest interior, right down to the worn chairs, is as it was when the famous architectural couple lived here.

Closer to downtown, **TAIDEKOTI KIRPILÄ** (Pohjoinen Hesperiankatu 7/+358.9.494.436/www.skr.fi/taidekoti) comprises a large
private collection of Finnish art donated to the Finnish
Cultural Foundation by Dr. Juhani Kirpilä (1931–1988) in
what was formerly his sixth-floor apartment.

Outside Helsinki, but Worth the Trip

AINOLA (Ainolantie/
Järvenpää +358.9.287.322/www.ainola.fi), the former home of
composer Jean Sibelius, is in Järvenpää, 38 kilometres
from Helsinki. Sibelius and his wife Aino, after whom the
property is named, lived at Ainola for more than 50 years

until his death in 1957. Sibelius and his wife are buried on the property. The house, filled with Sibelius memorabilia, is best reached by bus or by taking the train to the Järvenpää station and then walking for about four minutes. It's closed during the winter months.

HVITTRÄSK (Kirkkonummi/+358.9.29.75.779/www.nba.fi/museums/ hvittr) was the studio home of renowned architects Eliel Saarinen, Armas Lindgren, and Herman Gesellius, whose lives overlapped in more ways than one. When Saarinen's first marriage broke up, Gesellius married Saarinen's ex-wife; Saarinen's second wife was Gesellius's sister.

The artists´ lives overlapped in more ways than one.

Built of log and natural stone, art nouveau Hvitträsk is remarkably modern given that it was built during the early 1900s. The main building was an architectural office and a centre of culture. In addition to Finnish artists such as Gallen-Kallela and Sibelius, Hvitträsk saw many visitors including writer Maksim Gorky, composer Gustav Mahler, and other figures from the international arts scene. Here at Hvitträsk, plans for the Helsinki Railway Station, the National Museum, and other prominent buildings were drawn up. Hvitträsk is about 30 kilometres from Helsinki; take bus number 166 or the train to Luoma or Masala station and then walk for about three kilometres or cab it.

More Galleries

Around Helsinki there are many galleries worth checking out; here are just a few. **HIPPOLYTE** (Kalevankatu 18B/+358.9.6123.344) mounts quirky photography exhibitions — a recent show called "Underpants," featured a series of pictures of the photographer/artist in his undies — as does **GALLERIA JANGVA** (Kalevankatu 18/+358.9.6123.743) in the

courtyard next door. Looking out onto one of the city's many parks, **GALLERIA BRONDA** (Annankatu 16/+358.9.611.426) has been showing top Finnish modern art — ceramics, graphics, paintings, and sculpture — since 1978; Bronda's exhibitions change every four weeks.

Second-floor **GALERIE FORSBLOM** (Pohjoisesplanadi 27C/+358.9.6803.700) deals in big Finnish and international names and is more commercial in its scope than some of the smaller galleries. **JUHANI PALMU** (Yrjönkatu 16/+358.9.649.465/www.palmu.com), one of the internationally better-known Finnish artists, owns several galleries that display his paintings and sculptures. **MUU GALLERIA** (Nervanderinkatu 10/+358.9.625.972/www.muu.fi) is a smart place to get acquainted with new and experimental art from sound to video and performance art.

Theatre and Opera The majority of theatre productions are performed in Finnish or Swedish. The **FINNISH NATIONAL THEATRE** (Suomen Kansallisteatteri) (Läntinen Teatterikuja 1B/+358.9.1733.1331/www.nationaltheatre.fi) stages classic productions while the **HELSINKI CITY THEATRE** (Eläintarhantie 5/ +358.9.394.0422/www.hel.fi/citytheatre) produces slightly more experimental work. The **SWEDISH THEATRE** (Svenska Teatern) (Pohjoisesplanadi 2/+358.9.6162.1411/www.svenskateatern.fi) tends toward Swedish-language performances.

As the language of opera is international, presentations by the **FINNISH NATIONAL OPERA** (Helsinginkatu 58/+358.9.4030.2211/ www.operafin.fi) are perhaps more accessible to a wider audience.

Several venues including the Finnish National Opera, the National Theatre, the Helsinki City Theatre, and the Swedish Theatre are closed during the summer. But in exchange, several outdoor stages feature summer theatre performances and festivals. Check *Helsinki This Week* (www.helsinkithisweek.net) for event listings, or go to www.hel.fi, which has a search engine in English.

Dance Dance crosses linguistic boundaries. The **HELSINKI CITY THEATRE DANCE COMPANY** (Ensi linja 2/+358.9.394.0318/www.hkt.fi/ dancecompany), under the artistic direction of Nigel Charnock, founder of Britain's DV8 Physical Theatre, serves up provocative modern dance. The **FINNISH BALLET SCHOOL** has a residence at the Finnish National Opera House (Helsinginkatu 58/+358.9.4030.2211/www.operafin.fi). For further information on dance performances around town, go to www.danceinfo.fi

Tango Finland shares a love of tango with Latin America. Every year a Finnish tango king and queen are crowned at the country's biggest tango singing competition in Seinäjoki, which is about a three-hour drive from Helsinki. If you want to find out more about the Seinäjoki event, check out www.tangomarkkinat.fi/english. Though you may catch some tango dancing at one of the outdoor stages in Helsinki during the summer, there are not many places that hold regular tango evenings. In the Helsinki area, **WANHA MAESTRO (Fredrikinkatu 51-53/+358.9.612.9900)**, features traditional Finnish dancing, including the *humppa*, a Finnish couples dance distantly related to waltz and tango. Evening dances are enjoyed by people of all ages;

daytime dances are popular with seniors. In the suburb of Vantaa, **TANSSILAVA PAVI (Honkanummentie 6/+358.9.875.2595)** is an outdoor dance floor open during the summer.

Film

With few notable exceptions, such as the award-winning work of Aki and Mika Kaurismäki, which has been especially popular with cinephiles in England, Germany, and France, not many Finnish films have made their way into the international cinema world.

Jörn Donner, prolific author (he's written more than 40 books), director, cultural commentator, and politician is to date the only Finn to win an Oscar, which he received for directing Ingmar Bergman's 1983 film *Fanny and Alexander*.

Hollywood's Renny Harlin is one of the best-known Finnish filmmakers abroad, though most of his work is more American than Finnish. He is reportedly working on a film about former Finnish statesman marshal Mannerheim.

In recent years, Finnish films have started to feel more cosmopolitan. Consider 2000's *Levottomat* (Restless), directed by Aku Louhimies and produced by Markus Selin, which chronicles the transient liaisons of an insatiable young paramedic. The cinematography is impressive, as is the scenery (it's filmed in the summer in Turku) and the cast is made up of a veritable crew of bright young Finnish talent, including Mikko Nousiainen, Irina Björklund, Samuli Edelmann, and Laura Malmivaara.

Movie Theatres

Helsinki has several cinemas and thankfully foreign films are not dubbed: They're only subtitled in the two official languages, Finnish and Swedish.

Mainstream films — from Finnish, Scandinavian, and European films to Hollywood blockbusters — are shown at Finnkino cineplexes around town including **TENNISPALATSI (Salomonkatu 15)**, one of the comfier and newer cinemas in the city, and **FORUM (Mannerheimintie 16)**, which is slightly older. The booking number **(0600.007.007)** can only be dialled locally and there is a charge of .66 cents per call. **KINOPALATSI (Kaisaniemenkatu 2)** is another megaplex and **MAXIM (Kluuvikatu 1)**, next door to Fazer, is popular for its wide, soft seats. Tickets for movies are usually 5 to 10 euros, depending on whether you're seeing a matinee or an evening performance.

Finland shares a love of tango with Latin America.

BIO REX (Mannerheimintie 22-24/+358.9.611.300) in the Lasipalatsi media complex, **KINO ENGEL (Sofiankatu 4/+358.9.622.4431)**, and **DIANA (Yrjönkatu 10/+358.9.612.3622)** screen films that are more art house than blockbuster, along with small-budget Hollywood productions. The **FINNISH FILM ARCHIVE (Eerikinkatu 15/+358.9.615.400/www.sea.fi/english)** requires a membership and shows cinematic classics and those with a cult following. One of the city's best indie cinemas is undoubtedly **ANDORRA (Eerikinkatu 11/+358.9.612.3117)**, owned by the Kaurismäki brothers.

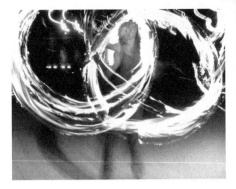

There isn't much in the way of movie listings in English or other languages, but you can usually figure out what movies are playing from the posters around town as the original title usually appears in the fine print. Check out the free brochure "Helsinki Clubland & Elokuvat," available in cafés, restaurants, and cinemas around town for movie times and listings. Although the brochure is not in English, you can usually decipher what's playing. As well, you can always ask someone: Locals are usually happy to help when it comes to navigating from Finnish to English.

Festivals From the renowned Savonlinna Opera Festival, to the Midnight Sun Film Festival in Sodankylä, and the three-week Helsinki Festival, which takes place toward the end of August, there are countless festivals scheduled throughout Finland year round. Helsinki's extensive array of summer festivals features local and international performers and spectators.

Festivals Finland (www.festivals.fi) lists most of the nation's music (almost all genres), opera, and other festivals. Though at last glance it didn't list some of the edgier festivals, such as fab electronic music and arts fest Koneisto (www.koneisto.com),

it does provide a good general festival overview.

The free glossy leaflet "Helsinki Clubland & Elokuvat" lists some festival events on at clubs and venues around town as does the free *Helsinki This Week* guide, and *City* magazine, which publishes two issues (winter and summer) in English every year.

7.

Sights to See and Stuff to Do

Out-of-Doors Helsinki is an eminently walkable city regardless of the season. Summer is more conducive for outdoor activities, but winter offers its own unique charm.

If you are keen on a particular theme such as everything Aalto, or the literary salons of 20th-century Helsinki, **ARCH-TOURS (+358.9.794.232/www.archtours.fi)** will customise a tour for you and your friends in Finnish, Swedish, English, French, German, Russian, Japanese, Italian, or Spanish. The **HELSINKI CITY TOURIST BUREAU (Pohjoisesplanadi 19/+358.9.169.3757)** also organises a variety of tours for Helsinki and points further afield.

Neo-Classical Nirvana Helsinki's city centre combines Russian, Northern European, and modern Finnish architectural influences that neatly illustrate the country's history under Swedish and Russian rule and post-independence. With the exception of the heart of Helsinki, much of the

city was built after 1917. In fact, 90 per cent of Finland's architecture was built after 1920.

The city's centre, **SENATE SQUARE**, which has been called a mini St. Petersburg, was created by Carl Ludwig Engel, a German-born architect, who combined neo-classical and St. Petersburg features in creating buildings around the square. Indeed, Engel had a hand in 30 significant Helsinki structures. Designed in the early 1800s, Helsinki's most photographed square reflects the Russian Empire's fascination with the glories of ancient Greece and Rome. Senate Square, which has doubled as a Russian backdrop in Cold War spy films such as *Gorky Park, Reds,* and *White Nights,* hosts popular rock and pop concerts and other events, drawing crowds of up to 70,000 people.

On the north side of the square, the **LUTHERAN CATHE-DRAL** (Tuomiokirkko), with its Corinthian columns and four cupolas surrounding the central dome, looms large above the square, atop 48 steps. A magnificent building in the daytime, the white cathedral is most magical at night when it's illuminated. These days its crypt is a café.

On the western edge of the square stands the ochre-coloured main building of the **UNIVERSITY OF HELSINKI**. Just up the same street, not quite on the square, is the **LIBRARY OF THE UNIVERSITY OF HELSINKI (Unioninkatu 36)**, which was also created by Engel, and is arguably one of his finest creations. The 1827 building with its lavish book-filled interior is magnificent both inside and out.

On the eastern side of Senate Square is the **PALACE OF THE COUNCIL OF THE STATE**, Engel's first monumental building around the square and the location from which Finland has been governed for the past 175 years. Here, Finland's only political assassination took place in 1904 when Finnish resistance to Russification culminated in the shooting of governor-general Nikolai Bobrikov by student Eugen Schauman, who then shot himself.

Further up the street, in front of the sombre **BANK OF FINLAND** (Snellmaninaukio), designed by Russian-German architect Ludwig Bohnstedt in 1892, is a statue of J.W. Snellman (1806-1881), who devoted his life to raising the Finnish language to the same legal status as Swedish. He was also responsible for making the Finnish mark replace the Russian rouble. On the base of the Snellman statue, you can see golfball-size pit marks, the result of a 1944 Soviet bomber blitz on Helsinki. Across the street, the neo-Renaissance **HOUSE OF ESTATES** (Snellmaninkatu 9–11)

143

has been restored to its erstwhile grandeur. These days it hosts meetings and official functions held by offices of the government.

Down by the Harbour Opposite the Market Square, the **PRESIDENTIAL PALACE (Pohjoisesplanadi 1)**, which Engel helped revamp when it was being rebuilt, is the official office of the president of Finland. Tarja Halonen, in power until 2006, is the country's first female president. You might even catch her walking down the street, *sans* bodyguards. Following the first three years of her term in office, Halonen had the highest public approval rating of any president: 89 per cent of the population supported her. When the president is in, the white and blue Finnish flag flies and uniformed military guards flank the gate.

Here, the president hosts the year's biggest social event, an Independence Day (December 6th) gala reception attended by 2,000 or so of the nation's VIPs, including war veterans, politicians, musicians, athletes, artists, writers, actors, and businesspeople. In the months leading up to the event, the media buzzes about who has made the guest list and what they'll be wearing. Those who don't make the list — most of Finland — watch the live broadcast at home. In recent years, there have been demonstrations against the gala as some people feel state money shouldn't be used for a lavish reception when there are homeless people on the streets.

Across the road from the palace is the **MARKET SQUARE**, a central feature of all Finnish towns, where you can buy fresh fruits and vegetables, breads, pies, pastries, salted and fresh fish, herring, and touristy items ranging from sauna accessories to Lappish dolls. This is also where the 200-year-old Baltic Herring Market takes place every October. Around this market square, New York artist Spencer Tunick photographed about 2,000 naked Helsinkians early one summer morning in 2002 for his "Nude Adrift" installation series that features nude crowds in different cities of the world.

Katajanokka

Just to the east of the Market Square and over the bridge is the neighbourhood of Katajanokka, with its regal Russian Orthodox **USPENSKY CATHEDRAL (Kanavakatu 1),** whose spires are visible from several points in the city. The red brick Byzantine cathedral with 13 golden cupolas is the largest Russian Orthodox church in Western Europe.

Katajanokka is full of gorgeously restored art nouveau, or Jugend-style buildings. This is the neighbourhood where artist and writer Tove Jansson, creator of the Moomintroll children's classics, lived as a child. On these streets, she played with a young boy called Poyu, whose real name was Erik Tawaststjerna — he grew up to be a music critic and the biographer of composer Jean Sibelius.

Central At the corner of Kaivokatu and Keskuskatu stands the **HELSINKI RAILWAY STATION** designed by the great Finnish architect Eliel Saarinen in 1916. Saarinen, part of the famous architectural trio Gesellius, Lindgren, and Saarinen, went on to achieve fame in the US, where he's credited with having an influence on skyscraper design — although he never actually built a skyscraper. Richard Rayner's 2001 novel *The Cloud Sketcher* is inspired by Saarinen's life and work.

One of the most famous public buildings in Europe, the Railway Station has impressive sculptures and reliefs, both inside and out, and fabulously large doors. At the second-floor Pullman Bar, the Helsinki International Press Club holds court. Outside on the platforms and up to half a kilometre away on the path around Töölönlahti, you can hear the magnificent echo of train arrivals and departures being announced in several different languages.

On the edge of the Railway Station Square sits the **FINN-**

ISH **NATIONAL THEATRE** (Läntinen Teatterikuja 1B), built in 1902 by Onni Tarjanne. The national theatre, which is housed in the building, began performing in 1872 in an effort to support the Finnish national movement at a time when Swedish and Russian cultural forces were strong.

Some blocks away on Mannerheimintie is the slightly foreboding granite **PARLIAMENT BUILDING** (Mannerheimintie 30), and down the street, the sleek, white **FINLANDIA HALL (Mannerheimintie 13E)** is a stellar example of Alvar Aalto's architectural mastery. It's also a venue for regular concerts.

The **KEKKONEN MONUMENT** in the park next to the Hall is a fitting memorial to the late Urho Kekkonen, the country's longest serving president (in power from 1956 to 1981). A controversial figure in Finnish political history, Kekkonen is nonetheless regarded as instrumental in maintaining good diplomatic relations with both the

Soviet Union and the West during the Cold War years.

The monument features a heated pond whose perimeter is shaped in a round, almost Aaltoesque line. On one side are four slender poles topped with sculpted bronze hands. Designed by artist Pekka Jylhä, the installation eloquently captures the essence of Kekkonen's political reach.

Parks KAIVOPUISTO ("Well Park"), possibly the city's favourite park, is in the middle of one of Helsinki's most exclusive residential areas, Eira. From the 1820s to 1850s, there was a spa on the seashore of Kaivopuisto, which is how the park got its name.

Walking up and down the surrounding streets is an architectural treat as the majority of the area's older buildings have been maintained in their original style. Art nouveau buildings from 1890 to 1910 line the seafront; many embassies, including the British, French, American, and Estonian, are on Itäinen Puistotie.

KAIVOHUONE, a restaurant with a summer terrace and a venerable nightclub, is in the middle of the park.

During the summer there are free concerts in the park — Swedish rock band Kent, the Beach Boys, and the Finnish Radio Symphony Orchestra have all played here. On the southwest side of the park, old-timers play jumbo-size chess.

Along the park's seaward edge, a boardwalk follows the Helsinki waterfront, with several cafés including **CARUSEL** and **URSULA** along the way. On a warm day, you can observe the Finnish tradition of mat washing. Using a fragrant pine soap, mats are scrubbed on the sturdy wooden washing racks on mini-wharves that line the shore.

The funky **OLYMPIC STADIUM** (Paavo Nurmen tie 1/+358. 9.440.363), built in 1940, hosted the 1952 Olympic Games.

You can take an elevator up the Olympic tower, which is 72 metres high. The view over Helsinki and the archipelago is quite spectacular, and the lean white tower is visible from various points in the city.

In front of the stadium is a statue of the great Finnish runner Paavo Nurmi midstride; when it was unveiled in 1952, the work by Wäino Aaltonen caused some controversy because it depicts the sports hero naked.

The Sports Museum of Finland is at the Olympic Stadium and the medals won by the flying Finn, downhill ski jumper Matti Nykänen, are part of the permanent collection.

In the same neighbourhood, some blocks away, you'll find the **SIBELIUS MONUMENT** (Mechelininkatu), a sculpture fashioned of some 600 pipes, in honour of the famous composer, Jean Sibelius. It's in the natural and unmanicured Sibelius park, which is meant to mirror the rugged nature of Finland, as inspired by Jean Sibelius's "Finlandia" symphony.

Sibelius holds a special place in the hearts of Finns not only because of his success as a strong Finnish voice in the world, but because he composed the defiant "Finlandia," (originally called "Finland Awakes") an unofficial Finnish national anthem forbidden during Russian rule.

TEMPPELIAUKIO CHURCH (Lutherinkatu 3/+358.9.498.804), designed by Timo and Tuomo Suomalainen (their names in English would be Tim and Tom Finn) in 1969, is built into the bedrock, with only the roof visible from out-side. Temppeliaukio Church holds services on Sundays in Finnish, Swedish, and English; owing to its excellent acoustics, it's also a popular place for concerts.

Cemeteries An afternoon stroll in the natural beauty and quiet of HIETANIEMI CEMETERY (*Hietaniemen hautausmaa*) on Mechelininkatu is a walk through 20th-century Finn-ish history. Alvar Aalto, Mika Waltari, Akseli Gallen-Ka-llela, and C.L. Engel are buried here, as are several Finnish presidents including Paasikivi, Kekkonen, and Manner-heim. A large memorial pays homage to the thousands of soldiers who died during the Second World War, and there's an elegant Orthodox cemetery within Hietaniemi Cemetery, which partly abuts the Helsinki shoreline.

The city's oldest cemetery is right in the heart of the city, in a square called the OLD CHURCH PARK (*Vanha kirk-kopuisto*) because the Engel-designed church there is the city's oldest. In the same block is PLAGUE PARK (*Rutto-puisto*) so named as the 1,000 people buried here — almost half of Helsinki's population at the time — were killed by pestilence that came from Tallinn in 1710. Nowa-days, the centrally located park is a popular meeting spot for locals.

Daytripping The following destinations don't necessarily require a whole day, but given that there's so much to do at the other end, an entire day could easily be spent. (See also Hvitträsk and Ainola under **Historic Homes**.)

SUOMENLINNA, a 15-minute ferry ride from the Market Square, was initially known as the Gibraltar of the North. Thankfully, the 18th-century fortress built on a series of linked islands off Helsinki is no longer in military use. These days it's a popular destination year round, though its numerous swimming beaches, cliffs, and parks are best enjoyed during the summer months.

Several art galleries and historic museums are on the islands, including **VESIKKO (+358.9.161.5295)**, a submarine-turned-museum, which was used in the Second World War and once torpedoed a 4,100-tonne Russian ship.

There's also a doll and toy museum, historical museums, art galleries, and Seawolf Studios, where major Finnish musicians and bands — from Hanoi Rocks to Esa-Pekka Salonen, Kimmo Pohjonen, and the Leningrad Cowboys — have recorded albums.

Locals often gather together a picnic from the Mar-

ket Square before heading over to these islands, but there are several places to eat and drink on Suomenlinna including restaurant **VALHALLA** (+358.9.668.552), **CAFÉ CHAPMAN** (+358.9.669.692), and the **SUOMENLINNA BREWERY** (+358.9.2285.030), which is considered by many to be Helsinki's best brewery bar. It's conveniently located close to the ferry terminal.

A UNESCO World Heritage Site, Suomenlinna is a great place to take kids; there's lots to do and it's relatively safe as there's no car traffic on the islands. Several hundred people — many artists — live here year round. Many of the gorgeous old buildings were created by architect C.L. Engel, who of course was responsible for much of Helsinki's neo-classical core.

Porvoo The city of **PORVOO**, Finland's second oldest town, is about 50 kilometres from Helsinki. Picturesque Porvoo gives visitors an idea of what a small town in the area was like a hundred years ago. One of the neatest ways to travel to Porvoo is by boat, the **MS JL RUNEBERG** (+358.019.524.33.31) sails to Porvoo from the Market Square. You can also get there by bus or train.

Founded in 1346 as a Swedish town, Porvoo was an important trading centre in the Middle Ages. Porvoo's sights worth seeing include the **CATHEDRAL OF PORVOO** (Kirkkotori/+358.19.661.12.50); the **HOME-TURNED-MUSEUM OF FINNISH NATIONAL POET JOHAN LUDVIG RUNEBERG** (Aleksanterinkatu 3/+358.19.581.330), who spent the last 25 years of his life here; and the **BRUNBERG SWEET FACTORY SHOP** (Välikatu

4/+358.19.548.4235), which makes great liquorice and chocolate.

Kidstuff   Helsinki is a child-friendly city. You can take kids and babies just about everywhere; pint-size seats and services for children are available in most places. Breast-feeding in public is completely acceptable.

Trams and buses have seat-free sections designed specifically for prams. Ground level doors on the newer fleet of buses and trams make navigating baby buggies on and off public transit an easy task.

You can get to the HELSINKI ZOO (Korkeasaari Island/+358.9.169.5969/www.hel.fi/zoo) by taking a boat from the Market Square, or by riding the metro to the Kulosaari station and then walking for about ten minutes.

Renowned for its success breeding snow leopards, the island zoo is home to northern European animals including reindeer, wolverines, and northern owls, and mammals and birds from Europe and Asia.

Off the other shore of Helsinki, SEURASAARI OPEN-AIR MUSEUM (+358.9.484.712) is also on an island, with some 100 re-assembled and authentically decorated houses from around Finland including a church from the 1600s and an aboriginal sauna. Take bus 24 from Erottaja.

Amusement park LINNANMÄKI (Linnanmäki/+358.9.773.991) was founded to raise money for the thousands of children orphaned by the Second World War. Today, the fairground has all of the standard attractions including a roller coaster, a Ferris wheel, some merry-go rounds,

theatres, restaurants, and cafés. The **Linnanmäki Toy and Play Museum** (Tivolikuja 1/+358.9.7739.9287) highlights the history of toys and features changing exhibitions. In the same complex, **Sea Life Helsinki** (Tivolitie 10/+358.9.20.320.320) gives kids of all ages a chance to see marine life up-close.

The **Natural History Museum** (Pohjoinen Rautatie 13/+358.9.191.28800/www.fmnh.helsinki.fi) is popular for its botanical, zoological, and geological museums, and its dating laboratory where artefacts are tested to determine their age.

The Finnish Science Centre, **Heureka** (+358.9.85799/Tikkurila Tiedepuisto 1/www.heureka.fi), features world-class science exhibits of interest to kids and adults alike.

Located in the suburb of Vantaa, Heureka is a 15 to 20-minute train ride from downtown Helsinki. (Take the train to the Tikkurila Station.)

8.

Let´s Get Physical

Activities   In Helsinki and its environs you can walk, swim, jog, bike, roller-blade, skate, ski, trek, sail, fish, and practice other sports.

Sauna   The sauna holds a special, almost sacred place in Finnish society. It's often (but not always) taken in conjunction with a sport such as swimming.

Essentially, a sauna is a dry steam bath, which can be made increasingly humid and hot depending on how much water you throw on the hot stones, which are heated electrically (most common) or by a wood fire. Contrary to popular belief, the sauna is not sexual in any way, even though it's taken naked. Men and women sauna separately. In earlier times, babies were born and the dead prepared for final rites in the sauna. The rules for the sauna are like those for church: One should not swear, pass wind, or otherwise act inappropriately.

Helsinki's only surviving wood-fired public sauna is the family-run **Kotiharjun Sauna** (Harjutorinkatu 1/+358.9.753.1535) near the Sörnainen metro station in the Kallio neighbourhood. Muscular ladies offer sauna-goers a scrub down, a bit like the treatment one gets at a Turkish bath; there are different sauna shifts for men and women.

Avanto Swimming

For extreme sauna aficionados, there are year-round sauna societies that practice the traditional winter dip in the water — *avantouinti*, or ice swimming — which is jumping through a hole in the ice for a quick swim post-sauna, even when the temperature is well below zero.

At the **Kuusijärvi outdoor recreation centre** (+358.9.874.3383), which is near the airport, a heated carpet runs across the ice to the hole in the lake.

Sauna holds a special, almost sacred place.

Most public saunas are paired with swimming pools or gyms. There are several sauna societies in Helsinki, including the **Finnish Sauna Society** (www.sauna.fi/ +358.9.686.0560), which is headquartered in Lauttasaari and has two wood-heated saunas, a traditional smoke sauna, and an electric one. Pre-booking is obligatory. Many sailing clubs and other societies have saunas on the islands around Helsinki.

The Finnish cottage experience is not complete without a sauna and access to a dip in the lake or sea. If you're invited

to a sauna at a cottage, don't turn it down — it's possibly one of the most relaxing experiences on earth. (See also **Sauna Bars** under the **Bars, Nightlife, and Live Music**.)

Beaches   There are numerous good swimming beaches on the shores of Helsinki. *Hietsu*, or **HIETARANTA**, is one of the most popular and is often packed on a hot summer day, with people staying on well into the evening hours when the sandy strip becomes an outdoor party lounge. **MUS-TIKKAMAA**, and the islands of **SEURASAARI**, **SUOMENLINNA**, and **UUNISAARI** all have good swimming beaches. As the Baltic is not too salty, a swim on a warm summer's day can be divine. **PIHLAJASAARI** island has a nudist beach.

Pools   As public swimming pools are operated by the city, a lot of indoor pools are closed during the summer months when outdoor pools and beaches are open.

Reminiscent of a glorious ancient Roman bath, **YRJÖNKATU SWIMMING HALL (Yrjönkatu 21B/+358.9.310.87401)** is the city's oldest indoor facility, founded in 1928. Scenes from 1983's *Gorky Park* were filmed here. Recently restored, the pool is surrounded by several labyrinthine levels where the changing rooms, steam rooms, and saunas are located. People from all walks of life come here, from business folk to old-timers, some of whom have been swimming here since the 1930s. Yrjönkatu is unique in that bathing suits are not worn; men and women swim in separate shifts. Saturday and Sunday nights draw a gay crowd. It's closed during the summer months.

MÄKELÄNRINNE SWIMMING POOL (Mäkelänkatu 49/+358.9.348.48800) is a new, large professional swimming complex with extensive windows to let in the light. Open year round, Mäkelänrinne has saunas, steambaths, and hot and cold tubs for a spa-like experience in a modern milieu.

STADIUM SWIMMING POOL (Hammarskjöldintie/+358.9.310.87854) in the middle of the Olympic Stadium Park, is a big outdoor pool open during the summer months.

160

Biking   Helsinki (voted the cleanest city in Europe) is relatively pollution-free, in part due to a great transportation system and a network of bicycle paths.

In the summer, the city turns into a sea of bikes as cycling is extremely popular and often faster than taking a bus during rush hour. Bike paths cover most of the city, and in many areas the paths have their own sets of traffic lights so cyclists don't need to jostle with car traffic. Pedestrians are quite well trained to looking both ways before crossing a bike lane, though tourists are not always aware that the bike path is for bikes only. A good ring on the old bicycle bell usually clears the bike lane quite quickly.

You can rent bikes from the Citybike racks around town in exchange for a 2-euro coin, which you get back when you return the bike to any of the 26 stands around town. If you're here for longer, there are numerous bike shops that sell new and used bikes, and the city's flea markets (see the **Shopping** section) often have pre-loved bikes for sale.

GREENBIKE (Mannerheimintie 13/ +358.9.8502.2850), in the VR Makasiinit complex, rents new bikes and sells used bikes that are in good condition.

Parks: Walking and Skiing

Nordic walking — all the rage right now — is essentially a form of walking with cross-country ski poles for added support and movement. This sport is practised year round, though the poles are particularly useful when walking during the icy and often slippery winter months. The **TÖÖLÖNLAHTI OUTDOOR RECREATION CENTRE (Mänytmäentie 1/+358.9.4776.9760)** rents hiking, camping, and outdoor gear, including Nordic walking poles. The centre also provides guided instruction, so if you want to try out Nordic walking, cross-country skiing, or something else, you can do so. Their prices are very reasonable.

HELSINKI CENTRAL PARK (www.hel.fi/keskuspuisto/eng/1centralpark) starts south at Töölönlahti Bay (circling the bay is a good half-hour walk in itself) in the middle of the city, and runs to Haltiala and the River Vantaa on the northern border of Helsinki. The park is about 10 kilometres in length, but there are over 100 kilometres of hiking trails, some of which operate as cross-country ski trails during the winter. Animals living in the park include badgers, foxes, arctic hares, weasels, and muskrats. A

diverse population of birds provides some excellent bird watching, too.

Skiing opportunities are numerous. Cross-country skiing can be done around the city — both on trails and on ice — downhill skiing usually requires a trip out of town. If you're here during the winter, check out **www.ski.fi**, which lists extensive up-to-the-minute info about all of Finland's ski hills.

Fitness Clubs

Private fitness clubs around town offer weight rooms and saunas, and aerobics, yoga, and other classes. Many clubs require a membership, though some have drop-in rates such as **MOTIVUS (+358.9.4153.3500)**, with numerous locations around town including Kaivokatu 9 and Stockmann. Its **ADLON** location in Töölö **(Runeberginkatu 44/+358.9.447.959)** is for women only. For the most part, instruction is in Finnish, although Motivus is one of the few gyms offering a few exercise classes in English.

FITNESS ESPORT (Salomonkatu 1/+358.9.586.8600) is one of the city's newer gyms, with excellent spinning machines and view of modern art museum Kiasma. **TÖÖLÖ GYM (Pohjoinen Hesperiankatu 15/+358.9.490.320)** is also well equipped, and is as much a place to be seen in as to work out in.

FRISKIS & SVETTIS (+358.9.685.4542) runs general exercise classes at locations around town. Men and women of all ages attend the club's free outdoor exercise classes in Kaivopuisto park (and other locations) on weekday evenings during the summer.

9.

Practical Stuff

The Helsinki Card offers discounts on transportation, museum and gallery entrance fees, shows, sightseeing, and a variety of other useful services. It's available at the **HELSINKI CITY TOURIST BUREAU** (Pohjoisesplanadi 19/+358.9.169.3757), **R-KIOSKS**, and other locations around town. Further details: www.helsinkicard.com

The Finnish Tourist Board maintains a WAP travel service in English (wap.finlandtravelguide.com) that is free of charge for anyone with a WAP phone.

MAPS of central Helsinki are included in the back of *Helsinki This Week,* which is free at shops, cafés, and restaurants around town. Many stores, such as Stockmann, provide free city maps.

GETTING AROUND

Transportation Public transit in Helsinki is relatively efficient with a system of trams, buses, ferries, and a metro that runs from early in the morning (5:30 am) until late at night (1:30 am).

The final run of the metro is just after midnight, and for trams, it's between midnight and 1 am, depending on the line. Thereafter there's a network of night buses that charge an extra night fare of 2 or 4 euros.

HKL, or Helsinki City Transport has a great website (www.ytv.fi) that allows you to type in your departure point, destination, and time and day of travel. In English (language options at top right), Swedish, Finnish, or *stadin slangi* ("city slang"), you are then offered several options, along with maps and transfer times. The journey planner is an invaluable resource if you need to navigate the city using public transit.

If you want to ride the bus, you need to flag it down as it approaches the stop. Locals do this by holding up their blue transit pass, which is a smartcard.

Within Helsinki, fares are between 1 and 5 euros. You can purchase single tickets on the bus, tram, or at the metro station. It's more economical to get all-day passes, strip tickets, or smartcards from an R-Kiosk.

TAXIS can be flagged down, or you can go to one of the numerous taxi stands around town. There's one adjacent to the Railway Station for example, though late on a weekend night, there tends to be quite a queue. (Queues are sacred here: Don't even think of skipping the line.)

You can book a cab by calling +358.100.0700. Taxis have an evening surcharge after 8 pm.

Tipping and Taxes In most places — restaurants, shops, and taxis — the tax and tip is included in the price. However, an additional tip won't be turned away. Doormen, bell-hops, and porters should be tipped.

MEDIA

Helsinki is a media rich city, but the offerings in English are much slimmer than those in Finnish and Swedish.

Net *Helsingin Sanomat,* the main Finnish daily, has a good website (www.helsinginsanomat.fi). If you click on the top right hand corner (there's a little British flag), you can

find select news stories in English and an archive of past articles. On the English page's bottom right hand corner, you'll find useful links for foreigners, though some of the listed sites are defunct, or not in English.

Virtual Finland **(virtual.finland.fi)** provides extensive information on just about everything to do with Finland. On the same site, which is operated by the Ministry of Foreign Affairs, NewsroomFinland **(virtual.finland.fi/news)** posts news in English, including domestic and international press.

For an overview of Helsinki urban life and history, and restaurant info, check out **www.aktivist.fi/inenglish/**. Alas, at this writing, their calendar of events guide is not available in English.

Other useful sites include the touristy **www.helsinkiexpert.fi** (click on the British flag) and **www.hel.fi/english/**, which is the City of Helsinki's English-language site. For up-to-date business news, go to the website of the main Finnish business daily, *Kauppalehti,* at **www.kauppalehti.fi/doc/eng.**

Print Helsinki's urban barometer *City* magazine brings out two English-language editions a year, though they are rather slim and much less juicy than the Finnish-language edition, which is published much more frequently. You can pick up the free newspaper in stores, cafés, and restaurants around town.

Published by the Helsinki Tourist Association, *Helsinki This Week* **(www.helsinkiexpert.fi)** is also available in the same venues as *City* and is one of the few publications that lists events and other information in English. At this writing,

Helsinki Happens, an English-language cultural glossy about Helsinki, is on hiatus.

There are several great trade publications in English, from literature quarterly *Books from Finland* to design magazine *Form Function Finland.* Check out the Academic Bookstore's magazine section for these and other titles. (See also **Books and Magazines** in the **Shopping** section.)

Broadcast

Finland has a dynamic mix of public and private radio and television broadcasting. The largest broadcasters are public service sector YLE (radio and TV) and private broadcaster MTV. Two of YLE's DAB-based channels offer programming in many languages: YLE World airs English programming 24 hours a day, and YLE Mondo broadcasts in a variety of other languages. YLE Capital FM 97.5 MHz (cable 107.3) offers round-the-clock news and features in co-operation with major international broadcasters such as the BBC, Deutsche Welle, NPR, and Radio Canada International. For further details, check out **www.yle.fi/radiofinland.**

169

Essential Phone Numbers and Info

AREA CODE: Finland +358 Helsinki: (9)
(There's often a zero in front of the 9, drop the o if you're calling using the country code.)

DIRECTORY ASSISTANCE: 118 (Can only be dialled locally, i.e. your mobile provider must be switched to a Finnish provider.)

EMERGENCY: 112 (Can only be dialled locally, i.e. your mobile provider must be switched to a Finnish provider.)

INTERNET DOMAIN: .fi

LOCAL TIME: +2 hrs GMT

MEDICAL CLINIC (24-HOUR SERVICE) +358.9.431.4444

MONETARY UNIT: 1 euro (€) = 100 cents

PAYPHONES: In Helsinki, it seems that everyone has a mobile phone and the phones are in constant use, either for conversation or text messaging. As such, payphones are few and far between. However, you'll find a row of them inside the Railway Station; there are also a few phone booths along the city's main thoroughfare, Mannerheimintie, for example, in front of Stockmann, Sokos, and in between the main Post Office and Kiasma, the Museum of Contemporary Art.

PHARMACY: There are several pharmacies *(apteekki)* around town; Yliopiston Apteekki **(Mannerheimintie 96/+358.9.415.778)** is open 24 hours a day.

POSTE RESTANTE: Elielinaukio 2 F **(+358.200.71000)** Open Monday to Friday from 7 am to 9 pm, and Saturday and Sunday from 10 am to 6 pm.

TAP WATER IS CLEAN AND SAFE TO DRINK.

10.

Index

Acknowledgments *A special thank you to Karen von Hahn, whose Toronto guidebook provided inspiration for this one; to Katja Turunen and Juha Salminen for the fabulous photos; to my family, friends, and co-workers, who provided support, valuable tips, and information; to Satu and Tapio Pantzar; to Riina Tamm, Kate Moore, Blaine Kyllo, Jaakko Soininen, Elisabeth Clement, Sam Hiyate, and Jeff Bickert for their invaluable input and editorial expertise; and to Pälvi Kuosmanen, Kaarina Joutsenniemi, Aleksi Siltala, and Jussi S. Karjalainen at WSOY for making it all happen.*

181

About the Author

*Born in Finland, **KATJA PANTZAR** has spent most of her life abroad, living in Vancouver, London, and most recently, Toronto. She has worked as a journalist, writer, and editor in magazines, newspapers, and book publishing. These days she lives in Helsinki, where she works as a writer and editor.*

E-mail the author at: hiphelsinki@hotmail.com

About the Photographer

__KATJA TURUNEN__ is an award-winning freelance commercial photographer based in Helsinki. After studying photography in Rome, she worked in Italy and the Netherlands. Her travels have taken her to India, Indonesia, Africa, and Central America.